even More
DeLIGHTFULLY Free

166 deliciously creative recipes free of

**Gluten, Dairy, Refined Sugar, Soy, Corn,
Yeast, Oats, Peanuts, Dye &
Artificial Sweeteners**

135 Grain Free Recipes

"Man does not live by bread alone,
but man lives by every word that comes from the mouth of the Lord." Deuteronomy 8:3

Tracy Hill

PHOTOGRAPHY BY CHELSEA ARMSTRONG & BROOKE ATTERBURY

www.DELIGHTFULLYFree.com

Even More Delightfully Free

deliciously creative recipes free of gluten, dairy, refined sugar,
soy, corn, yeast, oats, peanuts, dye & artificial sweeteners

Delightfully Free Press
Cover Design by Tracy Hill & Alan Hill

To order this title visit: www.delightfullyfree.com or call (714) 758-5727

Hill, Tracy
Even More Delightfully Free, deliciously creative recipes free of gluten, dairy, refined sugar, soy, corn, yeast, oats, peanuts, dye & artificial sweeteners / by Tracy Hill.
188 pages
Includes index
ISBN-10: 978-0-9849383-2-2
2016
Printed in China by Toppan Printing Company Inc.

I feel such gratitude to those, who have helped tremendously in producing this book.

My wonderful husband and partner, Brian, who whole-heartedly supported me by devoting himself to work side-by-side with me for countless hours. His commitment, companionship, advice & skills have been indispensable.

My three daughters, Chelsea, Brooke and Paige, who among their other many talents, are excellent, capable cooks and collaborate with me in the fun and creativity of developing recipes. Chelsea and Brooke also for their amazing photography. All three of them are precious and an inspiration to me.

My brother-in-law Alan, to whom I owe so much, for sharing his extensive technical and production skills, laboring over each page to diligently and patiently accomplish my many requests.

To my Mom, Dixie, for girding me with her prayers and support. For the enthusiastic encouragement of my family and dear friends.

And my utmost thanks is to God, Who inspired, enabled and blessed this work.

In Praise of *Delightfully Free...*

I made my Starbuck's® pumpkin bread-addicted son a loaf of YOUR pumpkin bread. He thinks it is even better than your brownies (which were off the chart excellent). He said this is now his favorite dessert. We love the cookbook.
Pam & Chris, Anaheim Hills, CA

Just bought your cookbook at my naturopath's office. Wow, I was so excited to see a cookbook with such delicious looking recipes that are gluten, dairy and sugar free...I've been on a constant internet search for recipes, but many times they add sugar when omitting gluten, or add dairy. You've put it all together.
Barbara, Orange County, CA

THANK YOU for your cookbook! It has been a godsend for us! A nutritionist we started working with recommended that we go gluten and refined-sugar free. I was overwhelmed and unsure where to start...then I purchased your cookbook! I am so thankful for your advice on how to stock your GF pantry and how to get started! My husband has always loved dessert, so it's been so helpful to have your recipes. The good news is that my husband is doing much better on our new regimen and we're enjoying really good, whole foods! We appreciate your contributions to that immensely. Our sincere thanks for sharing all you have learned to meet your family's health needs.
Julie, Minneapolis, MN

I reluctantly, yet enthusiastically gave my original copy of *Delightfully Free* to my daughter...she has a 6 month old little girl and is attempting to raise her on the foods that I, in my ignorance, didn't. She said she is in love with your cookbook...THRILLED is putting it mildly.
Tracy, via the internet

I'm playing my way through your delightful cookbook and cannot possibly thank you enough for writing it. Your Chicken de Provence and Black Bean Brownie recipes are outstanding.
Sarah, via the internet

I skimmed through your book and was HOOKED. With great difficulty, I gave mine to my daughter and had to order myself and my other daughter one. I cannot wait to get my hands back on that book.
An enthusiastic Mother in Davenport, IA

I made the Spiced Breakfast Bake to take to my community group and no one could believe it was gluten, diary AND sugar free! Not to mention packed with protein and slow carbs, thanks to the beans. Working full time in New York City and commuting to a job, I will do just about anything to save time in the mornings. I have found the Spiced Breakfast Bake is the perfect recipe for doing just that! I make it on Sundays and enjoy it and an extra 30 minutes sleep all week long! It's easy to make (even in a tiny NYC kitchen) and the perfect on-the-go breakfast or snack. A total crowd pleaser.
Sydney, New York, NY

Your book is a blessing to me! I used to pick up food or microwave meals. Now, I have people tell me I should open a restaurant when they taste the things I make from your cookbook, and they have no idea they aren't getting the usual garbage that's loaded in our food.
Shannon, Newport Beach, CA

Thank you for the delicious recipes in *Delightfully Free!* I have tried several soups along with the Rosemary Rolls, Lasagna, Chicken Enchilada Casserole, salads, side dishes and desserts!! Hard to believe they're gluten, dairy and sugar free. Delish!!
Lisa, via the internet

I just had a birthday dinner and my family made me the Pesto Pasta & Asparagus with the Cauliflower Cream Sauce. It was delicious!! Everyone loved both the main dish and the side!
Amber, via the internet

Today I used your cookbook for the first time to make the Chocolate Cake recipe. All I can say is WOW! I made cupcakes for my Mom for her birthday. I am not even going to tell my family that they are GF. I cannot tell the difference. I have tried just about every GF cake recipe and nothing comes close to yours.
Andrea, via the internet

I've only been gluten and dairy free for a few months but have longed for brownies that tasted chocolatey and fudgy like what I was used to having in the past so the first recipe I wanted to try was your Black Bean Brownies. I'll admit I was hesitant, due to the main ingredient...but they came out so amazingly good! My boyfriend, who can eat anything, thinks they're great as well.
Jen, Phoenix, AZ

We were eating breakfast at Tonic in Rochester, MN when I saw your cookbook on their shelf. What pure delight! Your cookbook is a godsend! Thank you so much for listening to and following your gut (pun intended of course)!
Barbara, Rochester, MN

We love the book and bought this one as a gift.
Jim, Scottsdale, AZ

Thank you for all the old favorites that you have made available to those who thought they would never be able to enjoy them again. The recipes are tempting to everyone even if they do not have any limitations. There is a great variety of main dishes, salads, pastas, poultry and seafood, snacks, cookies, and desserts to complete any meal. I especially like the vegetarian and vegan varieties. Your book is a great source for people with food allergies as well. As a nutritionist, I have to make recommendations that eliminate or restrict certain foods to resolve health challenges. You have done the hard work creating and testing delicious, healthy recipes for the entire family to enjoy. I'm happy to recommend *Delightfully Free*.
Dee, PhD, C.N.C., Irvine, CA

Foreword

As a naturopathic and chiropractic physician with two clinics in the greater Chicago area, I see men, women and children of all ages with a wide range of conditions. My specialty is natural primary care medicine. Clinical nutrition is an important part of my practice for restoring and maintaining health. Correct nutrition provides the body with essential building blocks to create and sustain health. The standard American diet is high in sugar, unhealthy fats, genetically modified grains, dairy, additives, dyes and fillers, while being low in fiber and nutritional value. This contributes to an onslaught of debilitating illnesses including cancer, diabetes and heart disease. In fact, 90% of illness comes from poor lifestyle choices.

For years as I have counseled patients, I have looked for nutritional support in terms of recipes and instructive, healthy cooking to help them improve their way of eating. Diet changes in themselves can be difficult and frustrating. Patients often complain that healthy food doesn't taste good and is difficult and time consuming to prepare. I had yet to find a resource that put that whole picture together, making it easier for busy families.

So, when I met author Tracy Hill and found that we shared the same philosophy of nutrition, I promptly began carrying her first cookbook, *Delightfully Free*, in my offices. As a natural physician, I believe that *Delightfully Free* provides an exciting, simple path to health. As an author myself (co-author of *Miserable Happy: Infuse Your Life with Genuine Meaning, Purpose, Health and Happiness*), I appreciate the quality of Tracy's book and the value of its nutritionally smart recipes. Also helpful are the beautiful photos in the book that show what each dish looks like. In every recipe, she uses creative alternative ingredients to replace dairy, soy, gluten, refined sugar and other problematic foods.

The feedback from my patients has been tremendous. They appreciate both the ease of following the directions and how delicious the food is. My patients and I have found *Delightfully Free* to be an all-in-one cookbook providing healthy meals for breakfast, lunch and dinner, including holiday dishes, and because *Delightfully Free* addresses a wide range of diet restrictions, each member of the family can enjoy the same meal, eliminating the need to make different dishes for varying needs. This frees up time for busy moms and dads. These recipes provide responsible ways for families to enjoy a wide range of sumptuous meals and desserts while still protecting and enhancing their health.

Now, I am excited to introduce the arrival of Tracy's latest cookbook, *Even More Delightfully Free*. This new book promises to be "even more" as it is filled with more beautiful photos and more innovative, delicious recipes. As a physician and a mother, I highly recommend both cookbooks, *Delightfully Free* and *Even More Delightfully Free*, to anyone interested in eating fabulously healthy food without sacrificing taste, variety and culinary enjoyment.

Michelle Brannick, N.D., D.C.

Even More Delightfully Free, My Second Cookbook

is the result of continuing to discover even more fascinating, creative ways to cook and bake the things we really want to eat, but shouldn't or can't because of the unacceptable, often unhealthy ingredients in them. I found that by using healthy whole, real foods as ingredients wherever possible, I could re-create these dishes. I have learned *Even More* delightful secrets to enjoy an array of even more fabulous main dishes, breakfasts, breads, sides and desserts—all guilt-free. Using the same technique, I've also included an exciting selection of **grain free** recipes (135 in all).

Most of my recipes are my own unique creations. In other cases, I've improved on existing recipes, such as the Cauli Pizza Crust on the cover. But, each recipe offers a very nutritious, clean take on loving our food and sharing that joy with our family and friends. As I have shared these dishes with others, over and again people are amazed. They shake their heads and ask "are you kidding me? This is made out of (...fill in the blank!) I'd never know. It tastes wonderful! Even the texture is remarkably the same!"

The emphasis of my cookbook is healthy, clean, delicious food which is free of ten problematic elements. **Every recipe is free of gluten, dairy, refined sugar, artificial sweeteners, soy, corn, oats, yeast, dye and peanuts.** In addition to that, under the title of each recipe are additional features. It begins with "Also" and, depending on the recipe, may include "Veg, V, Grain Free, Egg Free and Vinegar Free" There are breads, muffins and cakes that are grain free, "Potato" Soup that is potato free, Spaghetti with Meatballs that is tomato free, salad dressings that are vinegar free, and "Peanut butter" cake and cookies that are peanut free. All of this can be accomplished by substituting a nutritious, better food for the problematic one traditionally used. So, pizza crust, potato salad and white rice (in say Chinese fried rice) is replaced by cauliflower or cauliflower "rice." Cream cheese, whipped cream and cheesecake are clean and guilt-free by using cashews ending up with amazingly similar taste and texture. Pancakes and waffles you could swear are just like the ones you used to love are grain free and what's more, completely nutritious by making them out of white beans. And the list goes on.

As with my first book and now *Even More* in this one, my goal has been to use the healthiest, most nutritious, smartest ingredients, remove as many undesirable components as possible and create delicious new versions of everything from breakfast to dinner, including dessert, snacks and holiday favorites. My hope is that this collection becomes a blessing to many, helping them to live

Even More Delightfully Free!

Stocking Your GF, DF, SF Pantry

There are a number of ingredients that make this kind of cooking and baking possible. I have added some new ones that are key to the *Even More* in this book. Each ingredient adds an important characteristic to the finished product. So, even if they sound foreign at first, once you have stocked them in your pantry, and are using them, their worth and function will become clear. Many of them (like xanthan gum) will last for a very long time because you only need to use a small amount in each recipe (½ to 1 tsp in the case of xanthan gum). Others you will purchase repeatedly because they are your new friends and allow you to eat the things you have been missing.

You don't need to purchase them all at once. Start with the ingredients you need this week for the recipes you have chosen to make. All of the ingredients in this book can be found easily in most local health food or natural food markets, including the ones that carry this book and my first book, *Delightfully Free*. The ingredients can also be purchased online. Here are some of the key ingredients which are staples in a GF, DF, SF kitchen. Most, if not all, of these ingredients come **organic, which I highly recommend. (See Tips p.8.)**

Low-Glycemic, Natural Sweeteners

In this book I have used a combination of only three unrefined, low-glycemic natural sweeteners. They are stevia, coconut palm sugar (in granular and syrup form) and in 10 recipes, raw honey. For diabetics and others who must limit their sugar even more, I recommend using the stevia with the other sweeteners as directed by their doctor or nutritionist.

COCONUT PALM SUGAR is a granular, natural, unrefined sweetener made from the flower of the coconut palm tree. It has fewer calories than honey or agave nectar. Not only does coconut palm sugar have a **low glycemic** index of about 35 compared to table sugar with a glycemic index of 68, it is actually a **nutrient-rich** food containing key vitamins, minerals and phytonutrients. It has a rich flavor, which is considered to be preferable to white or brown sugar. In cooking and baking, it behaves much like traditional sugar, and so allows for easy substitution and the same desired results.

COCONUT NECTAR is a sweet syrup which, like coconut palm sugar, is the unprocessed "sap" of the coconut tree blossom. Though they come from the coconut tree, they do not have a coconut flavor. Like coconut palm sugar, coconut nectar is nutrient-dense, with 17 amino acids, vitamin C, broad-spectrum B vitamins and a neutral pH. Both the granular and the syrup have a **low-glycemic index of 35, are raw, unprocessed, high in nutrients** and have a delicious flavor, making them superior to other natural sweeteners.

STEVIA is an all natural, plant-derived sweetener which comes in liquid or powder form. I use it in the liquid form. It is intensely sweet, 200-300 times more than table sugar, although it is **not a sugar.** Stevia has no calories and a glycemic index of zero. Because it can have a bitter aftertaste if too much is used, I use it in combination with coconut palm sugar and coconut nectar to cut down even the amount of natural sugar in my recipes. It is important to measure stevia accurately because it can overpower and ruin the dish.

RAW HONEY In the few instances where honey is called for, it is used only in a recipe which is not cooked. Always use raw, which is preferable for a variety of reasons. Most importantly, it is unprocessed and scores between 30-40 on the glycemic index compared to processed honeys which score between 55-80.

Flours

There are many GF flours and meals. I have listed only the ones used in this book. I recommend keeping them in sealed containers and refrigerated or frozen for freshness.

ALMOND FLOUR is made entirely from finely ground almonds. Almonds are an amazingly beneficial, nutritious, whole food packed with protein, vitamin E, monounsaturated (good) fats, minerals, calcium and fiber. In baking, almond flour is a wonderfully nutritious way to make breads, muffins and cakes **grain free.** Almond flour is different from almond meal. It is blanched and has a finer texture. So, it results in a softer, lighter, fluffier baked good than that from almond meal and can be substituted for almond meal in breads, cakes and cookies but not in crumbles and toppings.

ARROWROOT FLOUR (also called arrowroot starch or powder) is a pure starch which is ground from the root of the arrowroot plant. It is a very light-weight, tasteless, **grain free,** white powder which works well to thicken liquids (other than dairy) without making them cloudy so it is especially useful when making a clear glaze or fruit sauce. In baking, arrowroot flour lightens and softens the texture of breads, cakes or muffins that would otherwise be more dense. It also acts as a binding agent.

BROWN RICE FLOUR (different from white rice flour, which I don't use) is unrefined, unpolished brown rice so it has a higher nutritional value and does not turn to sugar rapidly like white rice. It still contains the bran of the rice, so it also has a higher fiber content. It has a slightly nutty taste and because its texture is a bit grainy, it produces a heavier composition in baked goods. It works well in muffins, cookies and crumbles. It can add crispiness and so is the main ingredient in my Basic Pie Crust.

COCONUT FLOUR is one of the most healthy flours because it is made purely of ground coconut meat, consisting of 58% dietary fiber and is very high in protein. It is **grain free** and contains fewer carbs than other flours and most of the carbs it does have are non-digestible carbs which have no calories. Ideal for baking, coconut flour has a natural, sweet flavor and produces a moist crumb, enhancing the flavor and texture of baked goods.

GARBANZO BEAN FLOUR is roasted, finely ground garbanzo beans (or chickpeas). Since it is 100% a bean/pea, it is **grain free** and packed with protein & fiber, a good source of iron and low in fat. This makes it a great meatless source of protein. It does have a strong flavor which lessens after baking, so is best used in combination with other flours.

SORGHUM FLOUR is a mild, sweet, finely ground flour made from whole sorghum grain. It is very versatile in baking and works in almost any recipe including pancakes, muffins and cookies. If used alone, it produces a drier, more crumbly texture without chewiness. When combined with tapioca flour or brown rice flour, for example, it improves texture and creates a fine crumb. I also use it in my roux for sauces.

TAPIOCA FLOUR is made from the root of the cassava plant. Ground into a velvety, soft, white powder, it is slightly sweet and **grain free.** It is a good thickener in cooking, and in baking it lightens and creates a texture that is more like those baked with wheat flour. It adds chewiness, and so is a perfect choice to use in pizza crust.

MEALS, GRAINS & NON-GRAINS

ALMOND MEAL is simply ground almonds, which are a nutritious, whole food packed with protein, vitamin E, monounsaturated (good) fats, minerals, calcium and fiber. Using almond meal is a wonderful way to bring high amounts of protein and fiber to baked goods which are completely missing in traditional baking, and to do so **grain free.** It creates a moist crumb and allows a better rise in baked goods.

AMARANTH is the tiny seed of the amaranth plant, even smaller than quinoa. It is a nutritious whole grain, used interchangeably with rice, pasta, couscous or quinoa. It is high in protein and contains 2 times as much calcium as cow's milk and 3 times more fiber than wheat.

BUCKWHEAT (BUCKWHEAT GROATS OR KERNELS), despite its name, is not related to wheat and is actually GF. Although it is usually referred to as a cereal grain, it is technically **not a grain,** but a type of fruit seed, related to the rhubarb plant. It is high in magnesium with 4g fiber, 10g protein and 0g sugar per 1/2 cup. It gives a wonderful crunch to cookies, pie crusts and crumbles, and is also ground into flour for baking. Look for Arrowhead Mills®, Bob's Red Mill® and Pocono® brands.

MILLET is technically a nutritious seed, **not a grain,** but it is thought of as grain because of its grain-like consistency. It is tiny and round, with a neutral flavor, so it can be added to a variety of dishes. It is high in protein (right behind quinoa), phosphorus, manganese, magnesium and other important nutrients.

QUINOA (pronounced 'keen wa') is actually a seed, and is technically **not a grain.** It is a complete protein source with all 8 essential amino acids, higher in protein than any comparable grain (5.5 grams per 1 cup cooked). It is also a great source of fiber and other nutrients. It makes an interesting alternative to rice or couscous. Quinoa flakes are simply a cereal made from quinoa.

OTHER INGREDIENTS

AGAR POWDER is a natural vegetable gelatin which can be used instead of the unflavored gelatin, such as Knox® gelatin, commonly used in Jello® and other aspics. It is derived from the jelly of various species of seaweed. Agar also comes in the form of tiny flakes, but in this book, agar **powder** is used. The ratio of agar to the liquid used is different than that of traditional gelatin, so it must be carefully substituted. Another vegetarian option is Veg-a-gel®.

ALMOND, RICE & HEMP MILKS are the three dairy-free milk alternatives used in my recipes along with coconut milk. They work very well in DF cooking and baking, enabling us to create creamy sauces, fluffier egg dishes and the same results cows' milk produces in baking. Almond milk, made from almonds, naturally contains far more nutrients at higher levels than rice milk, made from brown rice. Hemp milk, made from hemp seeds, is particularly nutritious, as it is high in protein, calcium, phosphorus and vitamins B and D. Plus, it is creamier than almond and rice milk. It is called for specifically in select recipes. The choice between almond and rice milk is preference of taste and compatibility with the recipe. All 3 milks come in "Plain" or "Vanilla" flavor and "Sweetened" or "Unsweetened". Note that for every recipe in *Even More Delightfully Free*, **"Plain", "Unsweetened"** is called for.

DF LESS-SWEETENED DARK CHOCOLATE is what I use in my recipes that call for chocolate chips and chocolate chunks. There are several brands to choose from which do not include gluten or dairy products in their list of ingredients, although some use equipment which is shared in the production of dairy products. Some brands come in the form of chocolate chips but others are available only in bar form. These we cut into pieces on a cutting board using the point of a knife. Depending on your emphasis, some of the chocolate options include:

- Chatfield's® Double Dark Chocolate Semi-Sweet Chips
- Chocolate Dream® Semi-Sweet Baking Chips
- Endangered Species® Dark Chocolate Bars
- Enjoy Life® Semi-Sweet Mini Chips & Dark Chocolate Bars
- Equal Exchange® Organic Very Dark Chocolate Bars
- Guittard® Dark Chocolates
- Lindt® Dark Chocolate Bars
- Premium Chocolatiers® Dark Chocolate Bars
- Scharffen Berger® Dark Chocolates
- Sunspire® Organic Bittersweet Chocolate Chips
- Taza® Dark Chocolate Bars
- Theo® Organic Dark Chocolate Bars

COCONUT MILK is not the liquid found in the middle of the coconut. It is the juice expressed from the meat of the coconut. One cup contains 38mg calcium, about 89mg magnesium, 631mg potassium and 240mg phosphorus. It also is a great source of manganese, copper and zinc. It lends a creamy, rich flavor which is fabulous for DF cooking. All of the recipes that use coconut milk in this book call for **canned** coconut milk, not the beverage. Be sure to note whether it is "light" or "whole" coconut milk called for in the recipe, and stir it well before measuring.

COCONUT OIL is the fatty oil that comes from coconut meat. Quality, raw, organic coconut oil is a good choice for cooking, frying and baking because it is heat stable, which makes it slow to oxidize and resistant to becoming rancid. It has a pleasant, mild coconut flavor which becomes a delicious bonus in some recipes and is undetected in others. Be sure to select unrefined.

GRAPESEED, OLIVE, SUNFLOWER & RICE BRAN OILS are used in this book for different purposes. Grapeseed oil is what I generally use to "grease" baking dishes, cook with on high heats and bake with because of its neutral flavor, affordability, and high smoke point of 420° F. The smoke point of an oil is the temperature at which it breaks down chemically into harmful toxins including free radicals. Olive oil I use for savory dishes and sauces. Opinions vary in the information regarding oils. I believe these oils to be the best choices.

CRANBERRY JUICE (100% UNSWEETENED) The typical cranberry juice sold in markets is loaded with sugar because cranberries are naturally quite bitter. But, you can purchase 100% unsweetened cranberry juice at health food markets or Trader Joe's®. Cranberry juice achieves some specific purposes in several of my recipes and in terms of health, it has tremendous benefits such as inhibiting bacterial growth to aid in preventing urinary tract infections and tooth decay, boosting immunity, fighting cancer and aiding in digestion.

GF PASTAS now abound in natural food markets and even in more traditional ones or online. More importantly, the choices in types of GF pastas have evolved to include better, cleaner ingredients. Choose from quinoa, lentil, bean, buckwheat and brown rice pastas. Some of the brands to look for are Ancient Harvest®, Eden®, Ezekiel®, Food for Life®, Jovial®, Orgran®, Explore Asian®, Tolerant® and Tru Roots®. For more options, see the delicious substitutes for pasta and rice on p.48-49, Pasta & Rice Alternatives.

GF TORTILLA choices now go well beyond corn which is inflammatory and flour which has gluten in white refined wheat flour. Happily, tortillas made from brown rice, quinoa, teff, and millet are sold at natural food markets and many traditional markets. Look for manufacturers such as Trader Joe's®, Udi's®, Rudi's® and La Tortilla Factory®. In addition, my **grain-free** Naan, p.55 is a wonderful alternative to tortillas. Spread them to ⅛" thick as they cook.

100% CRISPY BROWN RICE is an unsweetened crispy rice cereal. It can be purchased in some health food markets in bulk. If you can't find it unsweetened, Barbara's® makes a version sweetened only with fruit juice.

EGG REPLACERS are an option for vegans and those with egg sensitivities. Three options are: **flaxseed meal** (1 Tbsp in 3 Tbsp of water = 1 egg, or as a fat substitute, 2 Tbsp flaxseed meal = 1 Tbsp butter or oil), **ground chia seeds** (1 Tbsp ground chia seeds soaked in 3 Tbsp water 5-6 minutes = 1 egg), and **powdered egg replacers.** Ener-G® brand is a reliable choice. I have found that the results are better if the mixture of the powder and water is whisked and allowed to sit for at least 10 minutes. Increasing the amount of baking powder and baking soda is also helpful. Replacing more than 2 eggs will change the consistency of a recipe. For recipes that use more eggs, you will need to adjust by slightly lowering other liquid ingredients and possibly increasing the baking time.

GHEE is clarified butter. Although butter is a dairy product, ghee no longer contains any casein (the protein in dairy) or lactose. It is concentrated, so a little ghee provides a buttery flavor in DF cooking and baking.

SEA SALT is healthier than table salt but has a less salty flavor, so it is important to use sea salt instead of regular salt in these recipes or you will not have the same result.

WHITE BEANS include cannellini (white kidney), Great Northern and navy. I prefer cannellini in baking as they produce the best results. I consider beans and all legumes to be a great source of nutrition, protein and fiber in fresh dishes and in cooking. When it comes to baking, incorporating beans into batters (sometimes even as the main ingredient) has resulted in wonderfully moist, light breads, cakes and muffins. Equally important, these breads, cakes and muffins have the fantastic benefit of no longer consisting predominately of simple carbs. Instead, because of their bean content, they consist of complex carbs and are high in protein and fiber.

XANTHAN GUM is an important ingredient in GF baking. Gluten, the protein in wheat, is what binds baked goods together and gives them their elastic, spongy quality. Xanthan gum provides this essential element in GF baking. It also thickens liquids such as salad dressings and sauces. Even though an 8 oz bag costs over $10, it goes a long way because it is used in very small amounts, ½ to 1 tsp in most recipes. The corn sensitive person should use a corn-free xanthan gum such as Bob's Red Mill® or substitute with guar gum.

Tips

Organic produce and products are so important to health and are always preferable. Fortunately, prices for organic foods have come down. Some types of produce are more exposed to pesticides than others, so these fruits and vegetables rank as priority to buy organic: all forms of lettuce, cabbage, kale, collard greens, spinach, cucumbers, celery, tomatoes, bell peppers, zucchini, peaches, apples, grapes, nectarines and berries. On the other hand, produce that has lower pesticide residues include onions, avocado, asparagus, peas, pineapple and mango. Choose organic whenever you can.

Every recipe in this book has been carefully thought out. Unlike traditional cooking, GF cooking, and especially baking, requires the ingredients to be measured correctly or else it really throws off the results. GF doughs are sometimes thinner, looking more like a batter. Crust doughs vary as well. Trust the recipe. The key to successful GF baking is to follow the directions exactly and measure the ingredients precisely using the straight edge of a knife to level each teaspoon, tablespoon and measuring cup.

There is a difference between wet and dry measuring cups. For accurate measurement of ingredients, use a wet measuring cup which has a spout for all ingredients that drip like oil, coconut nectar and DF milk. Use a dry measuring cup which has a flat top for dry ingredients like flours, lentils and chopped vegetables in order to use the straight edge of a knife to level off the top.

You will save a lot of time and frustration by reading the whole recipe before starting. This way, you will have ingredients like vegetables peeled, chopped and ready to be added at the right moment instead of delaying time-sensitive steps and changing the end result. In addition to reading the recipe all the way through before starting, be sure to follow the recipe exactly. Attention to detail in GF, DF, SF cooking and baking produces the best results.

To maximize time for busy households, I have included several casseroles. They make enough to provide dinner on a second night. The stews, soups and lentil quinoa sides, etc. were created with the same goal in mind. One of the great, practical benefits of my baked goods is that they freeze exceptionally well. So, when a recipe yields more than you use, freeze the remainder for later. Also a good time saver, bake a double batch or 2 loaves, etc., freezing one for later.

Other Tools You Will Need

A good **standard blender** or food processor is essential for the cakes, frostings, pies, soups, sauces and egg dishes as well as many other recipes. I find that a standard blender works very well for most of these purposes and using a blender or food processor does make a recipe quick and simple. An immersion blender is even better for certain recipes like the brownies.

For some recipes, a **high-speed blender** is required. These recipes are marked clearly with a high-speed blender icon at the top of the recipe.

A silicone spatula saves so much time and is vastly more efficient at getting the batter, frosting, soup, etc. out of the blender and even the mixing bowls.

Parchment paper is necessary for lining the bottom of bread and cake pans.

An oil mister is great and economical for spraying baking pans and dishes. Also, a mister is best for preparing the tortillas in several of the recipes.

In addition to the typical measuring spoons, a ⅟₁₆, ⅛, ⅓ and 1½ tsp (which = ½ Tbsp) measures are very helpful and will save you time.

A wire mesh strainer is necessary for draining beans, rinsing grains and even works as a substitute for a flour sifter if you don't have one.

A small and a large wire whisk are needed for whisking eggs and sauces, and also for whisking flours and other dry ingredients together, blending and separating them much like a sifter.

Main Dishes

CHICKEN POT PIE

Makes 4 Two Cup Ramekins   (w/ or w/o top crusts)

1¼ cups peeled, diced
    Yukon gold potatoes
¾ cup peeled, sliced carrots
½ cup sliced celery
1 cup chopped brown onion
⅓ cup olive oil
⅓ cup + 2 Tbsp sorghum flour
⅔ cup unsweetened rice or almond milk

3 cups chicken stock or broth
1½ tsp sea salt
¼ cup fresh thyme or 1½ tsp dried
1 Tbsp + 2 tsp fresh sage or 1½ tsp dried
½ tsp black pepper
3 cups cooked, torn chicken
⅔ cup frozen peas
• crust, recipe below

In a 2-qt pot, bring potatoes, carrots and 3 cups water to a boil. Lower heat, cover and cook 4 minutes, just until vegetables are crisp-tender. Drain, refill with cold water and drain again. Set vegetables aside on a paper towel. In a 4-qt pot, cook onion, celery, thyme and sage in the oil, covered 10 minutes on low heat. Remove from heat and cool 5 minutes. Stir in flour and ⅓ cup milk till well blended. Return to medium-low heat. Stirring constantly, as sauce bubbles and thickens, add remaining milk and broth a little at a time till all has been used. Remove from heat. Stir in salt, pepper, chicken, peas and potato-carrot mixture.

Savory Nut Crust:

Makes 4 Ramekins, w/o Top Crust (For Top Crust, Double Amounts)

2⅔ cups brown rice flour
½   cup almond meal
¼   cup + 2 Tbsp tapioca flour
2¼ tsp sea salt
1½ tsp xanthan gum
2   Tbsp + 6 Tbsp coconut oil
2   Tbsp minced fresh sage or 1 tsp ground
2   Tbsp minced fresh thyme or 2 tsp dried

2   cloves garlic, pressed, or 2¼ tsp powder
4   eggs
¼   cup water
⅓   cup + 2 tsp dehydrated minced onion
⅔   cup finely chopped almonds
⅔   cup finely chopped walnuts
•   parchment paper

In a small skillet, cook the fresh sage, thyme and garlic in 2-3 Tbsp of the oil over very low heat 2 minutes. Remove from heat and set aside. (If using dried herbs and garlic, add them to flour mixture.) Preheat oven to 350º. Brush 4 two cup ramekins with grapeseed oil. In a large bowl, whisk together the 2 flours, almond meal, (herbs, if using dried), salt and xanthan gum. With a large spoon, mix remaining oil into flour mixture, till evenly mixed. In a medium bowl, whisk eggs, water and minced onion. Add egg mixture and herbs from skillet with all of the oil they cooked in into the flour mixture. Press and stir until texture is consistent. Stir in nuts.

Divide the dough into 4 even lumps. Press dough into ramekins, making the edges a little thicker. Fill crusts with chicken mixture. Place ramekins on a rimmed baking sheet and bake 32-34 minutes, till crust is deep golden.

For pies with top crusts, double crust recipe, divide dough into two equal lumps. Use one lump to press into ramekins as directed above. Divide the other half into 4 additional lumps and roll them one at a time between two sheets of parchment paper to ⅛" thick. Remove paper, transfer to top of each pie and press/pinch edges. Place ramekins on a rimmed baking sheet and bake 36-38 minutes, till crust is deep golden.

Almond Chicken Francais

Serves 6-8   Also Grain Free*, Egg Free

2½	cups Cashew Cheese, p.129
12	oz French green beans, cut 1½"
⅓	cup dry white wine
2	Tbsp minced fresh dill
2	Tbsp minced fresh parsley
½	tsp garlic powder
½	tsp sea salt
2	dashes white pepper
4½	cups cooked chicken, cut into ½"x1" pieces
1	cup raw, slivered almonds
10	oz gluten-free or grain-free pasta, (p.48-49)*, cooked al dente and well drained

I love this dish! The combination of the wine, "cheese," dill and almonds makes my mouth water. I've made this recipe since I was a young bride, but back then, it was full of gluten-laced pasta and dairy in the form of yogurt and cheese. Now, it's new & improved, & I'm Delighted with the results!

In a 3-qt pot, cook the green beans in 4 cups boiling water only 3 minutes. Rinse with cold water, drain well on a paper towel and set aside. In a small bowl, stir the wine, dill, parsley, garlic powder, salt and pepper into the Cashew Cheese.

Preheat oven to 350º. Brush a 9x13 baking dish with grapeseed oil. Layer into the baking dish: ½ of the pasta, ½ of the beans, ½ of the chicken, ½ of the sauce and ½ of the almonds. Repeat the layers. Cover and bake 25-30 minutes or until heated thru. Uncover and bake another 3-4 minutes, just to toast the almonds. Remove from oven and allow to set 8 minutes.

Chipotle Casserole
Serves 8   Also Egg Free

1	small kabocha squash -or- 16 oz summer squash

Sauce:

1	cup plain, unsweetened hemp milk
2	15 oz cans white beans (cannellini, navy or Great Northern), rinsed and well drained
¼	cup water
1½	Tbsp olive oil
1¼	tsp sea salt
1	large clove garlic
2	Tbsp coconut palm sugar
1½-2	tsp chipotle powder, to taste

Filling:

1	large yellow onion, chopped, about 3 cups
2	Tbsp olive oil
1	lb ground turkey or chicken
1¾	tsp sea salt
1¾-2¼	tsp chipotle powder, to taste
½	tsp GF liquid smoke, such as Wright's®
2	Tbsp coconut palm sugar
4	GF, corn-free tortillas, see p.6
2	cups baby kale or torn kale leaves

For kabocha squash, cut in half and bake cut side down in a baking dish with 1½" water at 350º 30 minutes. Cool, peel and slice into ¼" thick strips. If using summer squash, slice ¼" thick lengthwise, brush squash and bottom of baking dish with olive oil. Bake in a single layer at 350º for 15 minutes. Allow to cool. Blend milk and beans till smooth. Add the water, oil, salt, garlic, sugar and chipotle powder, and blend till creamy. In a skillet, stir and cook the onion in the 2 Tbsp oil 5 minutes on medium-high heat. Remove 1 cup of the onion and reserve. Add the turkey to the skillet and the 1¾ tsp salt, 1¾-2¼ tsp chipotle powder, liquid smoke and sugar, stirring often. Cover when not stirring. Cook 8-10 minutes, until the meat is no longer pink. Drain any liquid, cover and set aside. Brush a 9x13 baking dish with grapeseed oil. Preheat oven to 350º. Arrange the tortillas in bottom of dish, trimming edges so they lay flat, making the layer 2 tortillas thick. Cover tortillas with the turkey. Pour all but 1 cup of chipotle sauce from blender evenly over turkey. Next, lay the squash slices over the sauce. Scatter the kale over the squash. Bake covered 25 minutes. Pour the 1 cup reserved sauce over the top and scatter the 1 cup reserved onions over sauce, or serve on each plate and then cover with sauce and onions.

Lentil Quinoa Stew with Butternut Squash
Serves 8-10   Also Veg, V (sub Vegetable broth), Grain Free, Egg Free

32	oz (4 cups) chicken stock or broth
½	cup water or additional broth
2	bay leaves
2	Tbsp fresh oregano leaves or 1 Tbsp dried
1½	tsp sea salt
¾	tsp black pepper
1¾	cups dry green lentils

¾	cup quinoa, any color
1	large clove minced garlic or 1 tsp garlic powder
⅓	tsp cayenne pepper
½	tsp cumin
¾	cup sliced black olives, optional
3-3½	cups raw butternut squash, peeled and cubed ¾" (about 1½ lb squash)

Stir all ingredients together in a slow cooker and cook on high 2-3 hours (checking after 2 hours), or on low for 6-7 hours.

Hearty & savory, a quick & easy, nutritious meal you can make ahead and also have several additional meals ready to go for lunches & other busy nights. Pair it with Olive Rosemary Bread, p.51 or Zucchini Muffins, p.63.

Cauliflower & Sweet Potato Chicken Korma

Serves 6-7   Also Grain Free, Egg Free

- 2 Tbsp coconut oil
- 3 cups raw chicken, cubed approximately 1¼"-1½" (about 3 breasts)
- 4 cloves minced garlic, divided
- ½ tsp + 3 Tbsp curry powder
- ¼ tsp + 1 tsp cumin
- ¼ tsp + 2½ tsp sea salt
- 1½ cups chopped brown onion
- 4 cups cauliflower, cut in bite-size pieces
- 4 cups sweet potatoes, peeled and cut approximately 1"x¾"
- 1 cup carrot, sliced ½"
- 2 medium bay leaves
- 1½ cups **whole** coconut milk
- 5 cups chopped Roma tomatoes
- 1 tsp coriander
- 1½ tsp ground cinnamon
- 1 tsp coconut palm sugar
- ¾ cup whole or chopped raw cashews
- ⅔ cup cilantro leaves + extra for garnish
- Cauli "White Rice", p.121
- Garlic Naan, p.55

In a large skillet, cook the chicken in the oil with 1 clove of the garlic, ½ tsp curry powder, ¼ tsp cumin and ¼ tsp salt for 10 minutes, covered when not stirring. Remove to a covered bowl. In the same skillet with juices from the chicken, cook the onion, cauliflower, sweet potatoes, carrot, 3 cloves garlic and bay leaves for 12 minutes, covered when not stirring. Meanwhile, into a blender, put the coconut milk, tomatoes, 3 Tbsp curry powder, 1 tsp cumin, 2½ tsp salt, coriander, cinnamon and sugar. Blend till smooth and stir into the skillet along with the chicken, cashews and cilantro. Simmer uncovered about 5 minutes, just till vegetables are tender. Serve over Cauli "White Rice," with Naan, garnished with cilantro.

So wonderfully flavorful & exotic, saucy, savory & fun! This Korma will make any dinner a special occasion. Incredibly good with the Naan or Garlic Naan, p.55 & served with the Cauli "White Rice" as shown in the photo. How Delightful that all of it is actually way clean, grain free, surprisingly nutritious & puts a "check" in the "eat-for-better-health box."

Lentils in Creamy Scallion Sauce

Serves 4   Also Veg, V, Grain Free, Egg Free

4	cups water
1½	cups green lentils
1	cup halved cherry tomatoes
1	medium avocado, sliced
1½-2	cups Creamy Scallion Sauce, p.133
1	extra scallion for garnish, sliced

This delicious sauce is one of my top favorites, a glorious marriage of green onion, lemon & garlic. The par-cooked lentils add a wonderful dimension, making the dish grain free, vegetarian and vegan, but with so much protein & so full of flavor, any and every type of eater will love it.

In a 3-qt pot, bring the 4 cups of water to a boil and add the lentils. Cook for only 9 minutes, just until the lentils have softened but are not mushy. Drain well. Dry the 3-qt pot and pour the Scallion Sauce into it. Heat it slowly over low heat, stirring often. Stir in the lentils and tomatoes, keeping the heat low. Once heated, serve with the avocado and garnish of scallions.

Cauli "Fried Rice" with Chicken

Serves 4-6   Also **Grain Free**

¾	cup finely chopped brown onion
5	Tbsp olive oil, divided
5	cups **raw** Cauli "White Rice", p.121
3½	Tbsp soy free, GF seasoning sauce such as Coconut Secret's Coconut Aminos® or Organic Aminos by Ultimate Superfoods®
1½	tsp sesame oil
¾	tsp sea salt
2	eggs, slightly beaten with 3 drops seasoning sauce & 3 drops sesame oil
2	cups chopped cooked chicken
⅔	cup finely chopped carrot
½	cup frozen green peas or fresh, cooked
½	cup sliced green onion

This is a treat. As good as take-out... Better! With all the flavor & color, it looks & tastes like the original, but happily, without any MSG, sodium benzoate, soy, or rice and greatly reduced sodium levels.
Just real food.

In a wok or skillet, cook and stir the brown onion in 2 Tbsp of the olive oil on medium heat 8 minutes. Stir in the "White Rice," 3½ Tbsp seasoning sauce, 1½ tsp sesame oil and ¾ tsp sea salt. Cover if using a skillet and cook 5 minutes, stirring occasionally. Remove to a bowl, cover and set aside. If using a wok, add another 2 Tbsp olive oil, adjust heat to low, and cook the eggs, chopping them into small pieces. Remove to the bowl with the rice. If using a skillet that does not have a non-stick surface, use a smaller pan with ½ Tbsp olive oil to cook the eggs, chopping them into small pieces. Remove eggs to the bowl with the rice. Add another 1 Tbsp olive oil to wok or skillet and stir the chicken, carrot and peas for 2 minutes on medium-high heat. Add the green onion and cook 1 minute. Add the rice with egg and toss to mix well. Stir and cook 3 minutes, then serve.

Pizza Casserole

Serves 6-8   Also Veg (w/o sausage), V & Egg Free
(w/ Traditional Crust), **Grain Free** (w/ Cauliflower Crust)

- Ingredients for either the Traditional Pizza Crust or the 13" Cauli Pizza Crust, p.43
- 1 lb sweet Italian sausage, casings removed
- 2½-3 cups chopped brown onion
- 2 cups coarsely chopped green bell pepper
- 1½ cups coarsely chopped orange or yellow bell pepper
- 8 oz sliced crimini mushrooms
- 2 Tbsp olive oil + extra

- 3 large cloves minced garlic or 1½ tsp garlic powder
- ½ cup torn fresh basil leaves
- ¾ cup sliced black olives
- 1 tsp sea salt
- 1-2 cups Old World Tomato Basil Marinara or Tomato Free Marinara, p.47
- ½ cup Cashew Cheese, p.129

Preheat oven to 400°. Brush a 7x9 or 8x11 (1.8-2 liter) baking dish with grapeseed oil. Follow the directions to mix either the Traditional Crust or the 13" Cauli Pizza Crust, but press crust dough evenly into the baking dish, coming up the sides of the dish and onto the lip. Use a square of wax paper to work with the Traditional Crust because it is sticky. Bake 16 minutes for the Traditional Crust or 40 minutes for the Cauli Pizza Crust. Remove from oven.

Meanwhile, in a large skillet, cook onion, peppers and mushrooms in 2 Tbsp oil on medium-high heat 8 minutes. Add garlic and cook 2 minutes. Remove from heat and stir in basil, olives and salt. Transfer to a covered bowl. Coat same skillet with oil and scramble sausage on medium-high heat 10 minutes, covered when not stirring. Drain on a plate covered with paper towels. Stir sausage into onion-peppers, and spoon into crust. Pour marinara over top and bake at 400° 20 minutes till heated through. Top with Cashew Cheese. Allow to set 10 minutes.

The family will dig in with glee on Pizza Casserole night. It's scrumptious, just like pizza. Make it with either the Traditional Pizza Crust (as in photo) or the Cauliflower Pizza Crust. The Cashew Cheese makes it "killer."

Italian Meatballs with Kale & Wine Sauce

Serves 4-5   Also Egg Free

- 4 Tbsp olive oil, divided
- 1 large yellow onion, sliced thinly
- 1 Tbsp fresh thyme leaves
- ½ tsp chili flakes
- 3 cloves minced garlic
- ½ cup red wine
- 20-24 prepared Italian Meatballs p.41

- 2 lb Roma tomatoes (a/b 6 med. size), chopped, or two 14.5 oz cans diced tomatoes, undrained
- 1 Tbsp fresh oregano leaves
- 1 large bunch of kale, stems removed, coarsely chopped
- 1½ Tbsp balsamic vinegar
- ¼ tsp sea salt
- ¼ tsp fresh ground black pepper

In a large skillet with lid, or 6-qt pot, cook the onion and thyme in 2 Tbsp of the oil about 5 minutes over medium heat, covered when not stirring. Add the chili flakes and garlic, and continue cooking 5 minutes, stirring occasionally. Remove from heat. Slowly stir in the wine. Return to heat and cook for 2 minutes to reduce. Add the meatballs, tomatoes, oregano and kale. Stir well, cover and cook 5 minutes. Remove lid and continue cooking 5-10 minutes until sauce is slightly thickened. Stir in the additional 2 Tbsp olive oil, vinegar, salt and pepper.

Yum! Zesty, saucy Italian food with all the flavor, complete with meatballs, garlic & red wine, but none of the starchy, simple carbs & that "ugh, I'm stuffed" feeling after dinner.

Poultry & Seafood

Thai Chicken Skewers, "Peanut" Sauce & Stir Fry

Serves 4   Also Grain Free, Egg Free, Vinegar Free, Peanut Free

- 2 large skinless, boneless chicken breasts
- Stir Fried Baby Bok Choy, p.115
- 6-8 wooden or metal skewers
- olive or grapeseed oil
- 4-5 cups Cauli "White Rice", p.121

3-6 hours in advance, with kitchen scissors or a sharp knife, cut the chicken into long strips, 1¼" thick. Into a 7x9 or similar size baking dish, pour all but a couple Tbsp of the Thai Basil Marinade, reserving 2-3 Tbsp. Stir and coat the chicken strips in the 7x9 dish with the marinade. Cover and refrigerate 3-6 hours.

After the chicken has marinated, skewer the strips and preheat the grill. Adjust flame to medium-low. Spray or brush the grill generously with olive or grapeseed oil. Grill skewers about 4 minutes on each side at 375-400° with the grill lid closed. Remove from grill once chicken is no longer pink in center.

To serve, make a bed of Cauli "White Rice" on each plate. Lay 2 skewers of chicken over the rice and a helping of Stir Fried Baby Bok Choy beside it. Serve with Thai "Peanut" Sauce if desired and the reserved Thai Basil Marinade.

Thai Basil Marinade

Makes just over ½ cup   Also Veg, V, Grain Free, Egg Free, Vinegar Free, Peanut Free

- ⅓ cup olive oil
- ¼ cup minced fresh basil leaves
- ¼ cup fresh lime juice
- 3 cloves garlic, pressed, or 1 Tbsp garlic powder
- ¾ tsp sea salt
- 2 Tbsp minced fresh ginger root or ½ tsp ground
- 1 tsp red chili pepper flakes
- ¼ cup coconut palm sugar

Stir all ingredients together in a small bowl.

Thai "Peanut" Sauce

Makes 1 Cup   Also Veg, V, Grain Free, Egg Free, Vinegar Free, Peanut Free

- ½ cup sunflower seed butter
- 6 Tbsp very hot water
- 2 Tbsp + 1 tsp soy free, GF seasoning sauce such as Coconut Secret's Coconut Aminos® or Organic Aminos by Ultimate Superfoods®
- ¾ tsp sesame oil (not toasted)
- tiny pinch of sea salt (less than 1/16 tsp)

In a small bowl, stir the water into the sunflower seed butter a little at a time, stirring until completely blended. Stir in remaining ingredients. Store any remaining sauce in refrigerator.

Chicken in Tomato "Cream" with Olives

Serves 4-5   Also Grain Free, Egg Free

- 3 cups cauliflower cut into 1½"-2" chunks (less than ½ of a 2 lb head)
- 3 cups brown onion, sliced ¼" thick
- 2 Tbsp olive oil + 1½ Tbsp
- 1½ Tbsp minced fresh oregano or 1½ tsp dried + extra for garnish
- 5 cloves minced garlic
- 3 cups chopped tomatoes
- ⅔ cup sliced black olives + extra for garnish

- 1¾ tsp sea salt
- ½ tsp black pepper
- 1½ Tbsp red wine
- 1 Tbsp red wine vinegar
- 3-4 boneless, skinless chicken breasts, cut into thirds
- • sea salt
- • garlic powder
- 4-6 cups of a Pasta Alternative p.48-49, optional

In a 3-qt pot, cook the cauliflower in 3 cups water, covered, for 10 minutes until very soft. Drain all water and set aside. Meanwhile, in a skillet, cook the onion in the 2 Tbsp oil on medium-low heat 20 minutes uncovered, stirring occasionally. Stir in the oregano and cook 8 minutes. Stir in the garlic and cook 2 more minutes. Onions will be golden with brown edges. Remove from heat and reserve ½ cup onion mixture in a small bowl.

Into a blender, pour tomatoes and cauliflower. Blend on medium speed **briefly**, leaving some of texture. Add the onion-oregano from the skillet, scrapping in all of the bits, and blend on medium **briefly**, leaving some of the texture. Transfer sauce back to 3-qt pot and stir in reserved onion-oregano, olives, salt, pepper, wine and vinegar. Cook covered on low heat, stirring occasionally, 20 minutes. Meanwhile, sprinkle chicken with sea salt and garlic powder. In large skillet, cook chicken in 1½ Tbsp oil over medium heat 12 minutes, covered, turning once. Drain juices, turn up heat and brown chicken by cooking just 1-1½ minutes on each side. Arrange 2-3 pieces of chicken on each plate, cover with sauce, garnish with extra olives and sprinkle with minced oregano.

Creamy Lemon Chicken with Onion & Capers

Serves 4   Also Egg Free

- 2½ cups cauliflower, cut into 1½"-2" pieces (less than ½ a 2 lb head)
- ½ cup chicken stock or broth + 1 cup
- 3 Tbsp olive oil + 2 Tbsp + 2 Tbsp
- 2 cloves minced garlic
- 3 Tbsp sorghum flour
- 3 Tbsp unsweetened plain hemp milk
- 2½ Tbsp fresh lemon juice

- 1 Tbsp dry white wine
- ¾ tsp sea salt + ¼ tsp
- 1 Tbsp minced fresh dill or 1 tsp dried
- ½ Tbsp minced fresh parsley or ¾ tsp dried
- 1 medium brown onion, thinly sliced
- 2 cups raw chicken cut approximately 3"x1½"
- ¾ tsp garlic powder
- 3 Tbsp capers

In a 2-qt pot, cook cauliflower in 3 cups water 10 minutes, covered, until very soft. Drain well. Into a blender, pour the ½ cup chicken broth and the drained cauliflower. Blend just until smooth. In a 2-qt pot, cook the garlic in the 3 Tbsp oil on low 2 minutes. Remove from heat and allow to cool. Stir in the flour, milk and about 3 Tbsp from the 1 cup of broth with a wire whisk. Heat on medium-low, stirring constantly, gradually add all remaining broth as sauce thickens. Remove from heat. Stir in lemon juice, wine, ¾ tsp salt, dill, parsley and cauliflower from blender.

Meanwhile, to caramelize onions, in large skillet, cook the onion in 2 Tbsp oil on medium-low heat 25-30 minutes, uncovered, stirring occasionally. Remove to bowl and set aside. Add 2 Tbsp olive oil to same skillet. Sprinkle chicken with ¼ tsp sea salt, ¾ tsp garlic powder and cook 8-10 minutes, covered, on medium heat, stirring occasionally, until no longer pink in center. Arrange chicken on a bed of rice, lentils, kale or pasta. Cover with sauce, onions & capers.

Halibut with Mango Citrus Salsa

Serves 4　　　　　　　　　　Also Grain Free, Egg Free

- Mango Citrus Salsa, p.133
- ⅓ cup olive oil
- 3 Tbsp fresh lime juice
- 3 cloves minced garlic
- 3 Tbsp fresh cilantro leaves

- ¼ tsp sea salt
- ½ tsp black pepper
- 4 6 oz pieces skinless halibut fillets, about 1" thick
- grapeseed oil

Colorful & flavorful as it is healthy, this dish is impressive to serve, but only takes minutes to prepare.

In a 7x11 baking dish, stir together the oil, lime juice, garlic, cilantro, salt and pepper. Dredge the fillets in it till coated, cover and refrigerate 1 hour. Preheat grill. Reduce heat to medium-low. Spray or brush the grill generously with grapeseed oil. Grill the halibut fillets 5-6 minutes on each side. They are done when they flake easily with a fork. To serve, place a fillet on each plate and cover with Mango Citrus Salsa. Pour remaining salsa into a small bowl to add at the table.

Summer Grilled Chicken & Vegetables

Serves 5-7　　　　　　　　　　Also Grain Free, Egg Free

- ¼ cup olive oil for marinade + ¼ cup
- ¾ tsp sea salt for marinade + ½ tsp
- 3 cloves garlic, crushed or chopped
- ½ tsp dried oregano
- ¼ tsp dried thyme
- 2½-3 lb boneless, skinless chicken breasts (about 4 breasts), cut into 3-4 pieces each
- ¾ tsp garlic powder

- 1¼ lb cauliflower, cut into 1½" pieces
- 2-2½ lb yams, peeled and sliced ⅓" thick
- 1½-2 lb broccoli, stems removed, cut into 1½" pieces
- 2 medium zucchini, sliced long way, ⅓" thick
- 10-14 spears of asparagus, ends removed
- 1 large yellow or red onion, cut into large wedges
- Any combination of these or other veggies

One or more hours in advance, mix ¼ cup olive oil, ¾ tsp salt, garlic cloves, and herbs in a large zip bag or baking dish. Add the chicken and mix to coat. Marinate in the refrigerator for at least 1 hour. In a very large bowl, combine the second ¼ cup olive oil, garlic powder and ½ tsp salt to toss the veggies in. Using just 3-4 cups of the veggies at a time, toss them in the garlic-oil and then set them aside in another large bowl or roasting pan. Repeat tossing until you have coated all the veggies **well.** You will probably need to add more olive oil, garlic powder and sea salt to the bowl.

Preheat the grill. Adjust the grill to a medium-low heat, approximately 375°, and spray or brush generously with grapeseed oil. Cook the chicken for 4-5 minutes on each side, just until it is no longer pink in the center. Remove from grill, cover and keep warm. Next, grill as many of the veggies as you can fit at a time on the grill using a pair of long-handled tongs. You may need to grill in stages since there are a lot of veggies. Keep turning the veggies, letting all sides become somewhat softened and grilled. Try to cook them only until they are crisp-tender. Do not overcook. Experiment with it and you will learn how best to grill each type of veggie. Remove the veggies as they become cooked. Keep them all together in the covered bowl or pan. This way, they will keep warm. When all is cooked, arrange the veggies and chicken on a platter and prepare to be amazed at how fast your family will eat up a huge mound of vegetables!

This is one of our family's favorite summer meals. But it is in stiff competition with the next night's dinner...Summer Grilled Veggie Salad with Chicken, p.101

CHICKEN WITH CREAMY BASIL SAUCE

Serves 4   Also Grain Free, Egg Free

- 4 medium-size skinless, boneless chicken breasts
- • sea salt
- • garlic powder
- • dried basil
- • dried oregano
- 1 15 oz can garbanzo beans, rinsed and well drained
- 1 clove garlic or ¾ tsp garlic powder
- ¾ tsp sea salt
- ¼ cup tahini
- ¼ cup fresh lemon juice

- ½ cup water
- 1 Tbsp olive oil
- ½ cup moderately packed basil leaves
- ¼ cup toasted pine nuts

Super quick & easy! This dish is wonderful served with millet, amaranth or brown rice, or for grain free, try lentils or sauteed kale. Looks fancy, but don't let the sauciness fool you. All the ingredients are clean, high in protein & full of nourishing goodness.

Preheat oven to 350º. Place chicken breasts in an 8x11 baking dish and sprinkle both sides generously with sea salt, garlic powder, basil and oregano. Bake 24-26 minutes or when no longer pink in center. Remove from oven and cover. Meanwhile, blend all remaining ingredients, except pine nuts, until creamy. Pour into a 2-qt pan. Stir and heat sauce on medium-low. Do not allow it to boil. If sauce seems too thick, add water 1 Tbsp at a time. To serve, place a chicken breast on each plate and cover with sauce. Sprinkle with pine nuts.

BALSAMIC GLAZED SALMON OVER SPINACH

Serves 4   Also Grain Free, Egg Free

- 1 cup balsamic vinegar
- 1-2 drops liquid stevia, to taste
- 2 Tbsp olive oil + 2 Tbsp
- 3 cups brown onion sliced ¼" thick
- 1½-2 lb wild salmon (enough for 4 fillets)
- • sea salt
- • pepper
- 16 oz fresh spinach

The rich flavor of the salmon with the sweet, spicy balsamic vinegar & caramelized onions is fabulous. Reason enough to love this dish. But, the nutrition benefits are also outstanding. Salmon is considered a top super food because it is especially high in protein & omega 3s, and spinach because of its antioxidant, phytonutrient & iron boost.

To make the glaze, cook the vinegar in a 1-qt sauce pan over medium heat. Simmer at a very low boil 15-20 minutes, stirring occasionally as it reduces to less than half the amount. It should be syrupy enough to coat the spoon. Remove from heat and stir in 1-2 drops stevia, to taste, depending on the sweetness of the vinegar.

Meanwhile, in a skillet, caramelize the onions by heating 2 Tbsp olive oil over medium heat. Add the onion and stir often for 20-30 minutes till golden with brown edges. Remove from heat.

As the onion is cooking, preheat oven to 425º. Brush a 9x13 baking dish with olive oil. Rinse the fish with water, pat dry and place it in the baking dish. Brush the fish with olive oil and sprinkle it with sea salt and pepper. Bake uncovered 14-18 minutes (depending on the thickness of the fillets). To determine when salmon is done, insert a fork and gently twist. As soon as it flakes, the salmon is done. While salmon bakes, coat a large skillet with 2 Tbsp olive oil and cook the spinach over medium heat, stirring often, about 4 minutes, just till wilting. Remove from heat and toss with 1½ Tbsp of the glaze. Make a bed of spinach on each plate. Place a piece of salmon on the spinach and drizzle with the glaze. Top with the caramelized onions.

Pasta & Pizza

Sausage & Brussels Sprouts with Fusilli

Serves 4-5   Also Egg Free, Grain Free*

- 1 lb uncooked sweet Italian chicken sausage, casings removed
- 6 Tbsp olive oil, divided
- 1¼ lb fresh Brussels sprouts (about 24), sliced in half
- 1 small yellow onion, sliced ¾" and then halved
- 1 small red onion, sliced ¾" and then halved
- 3 cloves minced garlic or 1¼ tsp garlic powder
- ¾ tsp sea salt
- 10 oz quinoa, brown rice or other GF fusilli, cooked al dente, well drained, or about 5 cups Pasta Alternative p.48-49

As delicious as it is eye catching, this recipe is so easy to put together, but they'll think that your culinary skills have hit the next level.

In a large skillet, with 1 Tbsp of the olive oil, brown the sausage 10 minutes by scrambling it on medium-high heat until it is fully cooked in large crumbles. Cover when not stirring. Remove to a covered bowl and set aside. In the same skillet, with drippings from sausage, add another 2 Tbsp oil and the Brussels sprouts. Cook 3 minutes on medium heat, stirring occasionally, covered when not stirring. Add the onions and continue cooking 5 minutes, stirring occasionally, covered when not stirring. Turn heat to low, stir in the minced garlic and salt, stirring 3 minutes. Add the pasta, sausage, garlic powder (if not using cloves) and final 3 Tbsp of oil. Stir just until everything is coated in garlic and oil. Serve immediately.

*To make this dish grain free, use a grain free pasta, or a Pasta Alternative p.48-49

Fennel Cream Lasagna

Serves 8   Also Egg Free

Sauce:

- 10 cups cauliflower, 1 very large or 2 medium heads (about 2¼ lb)
- ½ cup unsweetened, plain hemp milk
- 1 cup unsweetened, plain rice or almond milk
- 1½ tsp fennel seed
- 2 tsp garlic powder
- 1¾ tsp sea salt
- 1½ tsp dried basil

Filling:

- 1 lb ground turkey
- 1 Tbsp olive oil
- 1 Tbsp fennel seed
- 4 cloves minced garlic or 1 Tbsp + 1 tsp garlic powder
- 1¼ tsp sea salt
- ½ cup chopped fresh basil leaves or 1 Tbsp dried

- 11 brown rice or other GF lasagna noodles (Tinkyada® is my favorite)
- 1½ Tbsp grapeseed oil

In a 6-qt pot, cook cauliflower in 6 cups boiling water 10 minutes, covered, until very soft. Drain very well. Into a blender, pour both of the milks and the drained cauliflower. Blend just until smooth. Add the 1½ tsp fennel, 2 tsp garlic powder, 1¾ tsp salt and 1½ tsp dried basil. Blend just till creamy (don't over blend) and set aside.

In a skillet, cook the turkey in the olive oil with 1 Tbsp fennel seed, the minced garlic, 1¼ tsp salt, and ½ cup basil leaves over medium heat, stirring often to break it up and cook it evenly. Cover when not stirring. Cook 8-10 minutes, until the meat is no longer pink. Drain any fat, reserve 1 cup in a small bowl, cover and set aside.

Use a wide pan (12" wide is best) to par-cook the lasagna noodles. Fill half full with water. Bring water to a boil, add 1½ Tbsp grapeseed oil and cook ½ the noodles at a time. Boil noodles gently only 6-7 minutes, or they will tear and be hard to work with. Remove noodles to a pan of cold water to stop them from continuing to cook. Drain and place noodles on wax paper to dry.

Pre-heat oven to 350°. Into a 9x13 baking dish, spoon a small amount of sauce, just enough to cover the bottom. Next, lay 3 of the lasagna noodles in the pan and "patch" in the area needing noodles by cutting sections off an extra noodle to fill in. Spoon ⅓ of the Fennel Cream Sauce over the noodles. Sprinkle with ⅓ of the meat. Repeat these steps 2 more times, beginning with the noodles and ending with the sauce. Top with the 1 cup reserved meat. Cover with a baking sheet and bake 30 minutes. Remove from oven and allow to set 15 minutes before serving.

A fabulous, creamy new version of lasagna. Serve at a dinner party or for the family. It makes a lot, so you can have 2 dinners in one.

CHICKEN, MUSHROOMS & CREAMY SCALLION SAUCE

Serves 4   Also Egg Free, Grain Free*

1	Tbsp olive oil
2	medium boneless, skinless chicken breasts, about 1½ cups, cut into 2-3" pieces
1¾	cups sliced crimini mushrooms
3	cloves minced garlic
10	oz quinoa, brown rice or other GF fusilli, cooked al dente, well drained
2-2½	cups Creamy Scallion Sauce, p.133
½	cup toasted walnuts, halved

Oh, the flavor! Tangy, creamy, green-onion, lemon & garlic sauce with savory mushrooms & toasted walnuts. If you eat grain free, substitute vegetables like kale, zucchini or spaghetti squash for the pasta. Either way, it's hard to keep from licking the plate when no one's looking.

In a large skillet, cook the chicken in the oil on medium heat, stirring often for 10 minutes. Cover when not stirring. Remove the chicken to a covered bowl. In same skillet with the drippings from the chicken, cook the mushrooms 7 minutes. Stir in the garlic and cook 1 minute. Add the Scallion Sauce to the skillet and heat slowly over low heat, stirring often. Toss the cooked pasta and chicken in the skillet with the mushrooms and sauce, or arrange the chicken on a bed of pasta, pour the sauce over top and sprinkle with the walnuts.

*To make this dish grain free, use a grain free pasta, or a Pasta Alternative p.48-49

WALNUT ROSEMARY CREAM SAUCE OVER "PASTA"*

Serves 4   Also Veg, V, Egg Free

2	Tbsp olive oil
4	cloves minced garlic
1½	Tbsp minced fresh rosemary leaves
3	Tbsp sorghum flour
1½	cups **light** coconut milk
1	cup plain, unsweetened hemp milk
1¼	tsp sea salt
1¼	cup toasted walnuts, coarsely chopped
12	oz GF pasta, cooked al dente, or about 5 cups Pasta Alternatives, p.48-49

The wonderful aroma & flavor of rosemary in this creamy sauce is just the beginning of why this dish is so good. Multiple benefits of this herb also deserve noting. The anti-inflammatory component in rosemary helps stimulate the immune system, improves digestion & increases circulation including blood flow to the brain, helping concentration.

To toast nuts, preheat oven to 350º. Spread nuts on a baking sheet and bake about 5 minutes, until light golden and fragrant. Allow to cool, then chop. In a 3-qt pot, cook the garlic and rosemary in the oil for only 2 minutes on low heat, stirring constantly. Remove from heat. Stir in the flour and about 3 Tbsp of the coconut milk. Turn heat on to medium-low and stirring constantly, continue to add small amounts of milk(s) to the pan. Each time the sauce begins to thicken, add a little milk, until both the milks are stirred in. Remove from heat and stir in the salt. To serve, either toss the pasta in the sauce with the walnuts or make a bed of pasta on each plate, cover with sauce and sprinkle with walnuts.

* The fusilli "pasta" shown in photo is **grain free**, made entirely of black beans and sold in health food markets. See Pasta Alternatives p.48-49

WHITE WINE DILL CHICKEN

Serves 5-6   Also Egg Free, Grain Free*

2	cups raw unsalted cashews, soaked in 2 cups water at least 2 hours, well drained
⅓	cup water
¼	cup + 1½ tsp fresh lemon juice
3	large cloves garlic
1	tsp sea salt
¼	cup dry white wine
2½	tsp chopped fresh dill + extra for garnish
3	medium-size boneless, skinless chicken breasts, cut into thirds
1	Tbsp olive oil + extra
12	oz asparagus, cut in 2" lengths
4-6	fresh artichoke hearts, halved, or one 14 oz can artichoke hearts in water (not marinated)
2	cups fresh spinach*
12	oz quinoa, brown rice or other GF fettuccine, cooked al dente, well drained

Creamy, savory wine & dill over tender-crisp asparagus & beautiful artichokes with delicious chicken look & taste like a special dinner out. Truly impressive, yet healthy & simple to make.

*To make this dish grain free, omit the fettuccine and increase the spinach to 8 cups

Sauce:

Into a **high-speed blender,** put the soaked and drained cashews, ⅓ cup water, lemon juice, garlic and salt, and blend on high speed, scrapping down sides when necessary, till fluffy. Add the wine and blend briefly. Stir in the 2½ tsp dill, cover and set aside.

Into a large skillet, put the chicken pieces with the 1 Tbsp oil and sprinkle with sea salt. Cook over medium heat, covered, about 10 minutes till cooked thru, turning over once to cook both sides. Remove chicken to a covered bowl. In same skillet with the juices from the chicken, cook the asparagus on low heat, covered just 4 minutes. Remove asparagus to bowl. Add the fettuccine, if using, and the spinach, still on low heat and toss. Add a little more olive oil if necessary. Make a bed of the fettuccine-spinach, or just the spinach, on each plate. Heat the chicken and artichoke hearts briefly in the skillet. Arrange the chicken, artichokes and asparagus on the bed of fettuccine/spinach. Cover with sauce, sprinkle with dill and serve.

New Carbonara

Serves 4   Also Veg, **Grain Free**

- 4 cups cooked "Spaghetti Squash," p.49
- 6 eggs
- 1 Tbsp rice or almond milk
- ¼ cup olive oil, divided
- 8 large cloves minced garlic
- 2 Tbsp minced fresh parsley + 1 Tbsp for garnish
- ⅓ cup sliced green onion + 3 Tbsp for garnish
- ½ cup chopped Roma tomatoes, optional
- ½ tsp sea salt, divided
- • freshly ground black pepper

A new take on an old favorite, try this dairy-free & even grain-free version. The spaghetti squash is fabulous in this tasty dish which is normally made with pasta noodles. This version is quick & easy, extremely low fat, low calorie, high protein, high fiber & just as good for **breakfast** it is for lunch or dinner.

In a medium bowl, whisk eggs, milk, ¼ tsp of the salt and 2 twists ground pepper. In a skillet, heat 2 Tbsp oil over low heat. Add the garlic, stir and cook 2 minutes. Stir in the squash, another 2 Tbsp oil and ¼ tsp of the salt. Adjust heat to medium and cook 3 minutes, stirring occasionally. Add egg mixture, parsley and green onion to the skillet. Stir and coat the squash. Continue stirring until egg is evenly combined and sufficiently cooked. Stir in tomato, if using, remove from heat and serve topped with parsley, green onion and fresh ground pepper.

Red Pepper Cream Sauce with "Pasta" & Peppers 🍶

Serves 5   Also Veg, V, Grain Free*, Egg Free

Sauce:
- 3 Tbsp olive oil
- 1 cup toasted** almonds
- 2 cups chopped red bell pepper
- 3 Tbsp fresh lemon juice
- ¾ cup water
- 3 cloves garlic
- 1½ tsp sea salt

"Pasta" & Peppers:
- 1½ cups red bell pepper, cut into 1" chunks
- 2 Tbsp olive oil
- 1½ cups acorn, butternut or kabocha squash, roasted, cut into 1" chunks
- 1 cup torn fresh basil leaves
- ⅔ cup halved or coarsely chopped toasted walnuts
- 14 oz GF pasta*, cooked al dente, or 5 cups Pasta Alternative*, p.48-49

*Grain Free with quinoa, lentil, bean or other grain-free pasta or with a Pasta Alternative p.48-49

**To toast nuts, preheat oven to 350º. Spread nuts on a baking sheet and bake 5 minutes until light golden and fragrant.

To roast the squash, preheat oven to 375º. Use a large, sharp knife to carefully cut squash in ½ lengthwise. Scoop out seeds. Place squash cut-side down in a baking dish sized to fit both halves with 1 cup water. Roast uncovered 25-35 minutes depending on its size, just until tender when pierced with a knife.

Into **a high-speed blender,** pour all sauce ingredients and blend until smooth, scraping sides of blender as needed. Transfer to a 4-qt pot, cover and set aside. In a large skillet, cook the 1½ cups bell pepper in the 2 Tbsp oil over medium heat 8 minutes. Stir in the roasted squash and basil and cook 2 more minutes. Remove from heat. Place the 4-qt pot of sauce over medium-low heat and stir constantly till heated. Do not allow to boil. Toss the pasta in the sauce and divide it between the plates. Top each with the vegetables and sprinkle with walnuts.

Fabulous, rich & creamy. It sure doesn't taste like it fits in the very healthy category, but see how clean & natural the ingredients are. Eating so healthy never tasted so good!

Tomato Free Spaghetti with Meatballs

Serves 4   Also Veg, V (w/o meatballs), Egg Free*, Tomato Free

- 3 cups Tomato Free Marinara, p.47
- ¼ lb ground turkey
- ½ lb uncooked sweet Italian chicken sausage, casings removed
- ½ small egg, or ½ Tbsp olive oil*
- 2 Tbsp fresh basil, chopped, or ¾ tsp dried

- ½ tsp fennel seeds
- ¼ tsp + ⅛ tsp sea salt
- ⅓-½ cup brown rice breadcrumbs, depending on consistency
- 12 oz cooked quinoa, brown rice or other GF spaghetti

Italian Meatballs (Makes 20-24):

Preheat oven to 350º. Brush a baking sheet with grapeseed oil. In a large bowl (I use glass or metal when mixing raw meat), mix the turkey with the sausage. Add the egg or oil* and seasonings, and mix well. Stir in ⅓ cup of the breadcrumbs. If mixture is too wet, add a little more breadcrumbs. Form 1½" meatballs on the baking sheet. Bake 20 minutes, just until the centers are no longer pink. Do not overcook. Pat dry with a paper towel. To serve make a bed of pasta on each plate, cover with sauce and top with meatballs.

They will never know! It looks like spaghetti sauce, it tastes like spaghetti sauce... but it isn't. It's 100% tomato free, made of garden vegetables. So, even if you've had to cut tomatoes out—spaghetti is now back in.

Pizza Spaghetti

Serves 5-6   Also Egg Free, Grain Free*

- 1 lb uncooked, sweet Italian chicken sausage, casings removed
- 1 Tbsp grapeseed oil
- 2 different colored bell peppers (yellow, orange, red or green), thinly sliced, about 2 cups
- ½ small red onion, thinly sliced
- 1½ Tbsp olive oil + 2 Tbsp + ¼ cup
- 1 tsp sea salt
- 4 oz crimini mushrooms, sliced, about 2 cups

- 6 large cloves garlic, pressed
- ½ cup sliced black olives
- 1½ cups chopped tomatoes
- ½ cup moderately packed, chopped fresh basil leaves
- 12 oz quinoa, brown rice or other GF spaghetti, cooked al dente, well drained
- 3 Tbsp chopped Italian flat leaf parsley

In a skillet, scramble the sausage in 1 Tbsp grapeseed oil 10 minutes until cooked. Drain well, cover and set aside. Preheat oven to 375º and brush a baking sheet with grapeseed oil. In a large bowl, toss the bell peppers and onion in 1½ Tbsp of the olive oil. Spread them onto the baking sheet and roast for 5 minutes. Remove from oven and set aside. In a large skillet, cook the mushrooms in 2 Tbsp of the olive oil on medium heat for 6 minutes. Stir in the garlic and cook 2 minutes. Remove from heat and add the remaining ¼ cup olive oil, sea salt and spaghetti. Toss to coat. Add the sausage, olives and basil. Return to medium-high heat and cook, stirring just until heated. Stir in the bell pepper, onions and tomatoes, and serve sprinkled with the parsley.

*To make this dish grain free, use a grain free pasta, or a Pasta Alternative p.48-49

Ever been dying for pizza, but you didn't have time or ingredients to make the crust? Solution: whip up Pizza Spaghetti instead. Every bite tastes like pizza sans the crust. Magnifico!

CREAMY PESTO PIZZA WITH CHICKEN & ARTICHOKES

Makes One 13" pizza

Also Veg (w/o chicken), V & Egg Free (w/ Traditional Crust), Grain Free (w/ Cauli Crust & Pesto)

Pesto:
- ¾ cup chopped walnuts or pine nuts
- 2 cloves garlic
- 3 cups fresh basil leaves, lightly packed
- ⅓ tsp sea salt, or more, to taste
- 3-6 Tbsp olive oil
- 1 Tbsp fresh lemon juice

Creamy Pesto Sauce:
- 2 Tbsp olive oil
- 3 Tbsp sorghum flour
- 1½ tsp garlic powder
- ½ cup plain rice or almond milk
- ½ cup coconut milk
- ¾ tsp sea salt
- 1 cup pesto

Toppings:
- 1½ cups cooked torn chicken
- 1 15 oz can artichoke hearts in water (not marinated), coarsely chopped
- ¾ cup halved kalamata olives
- 2½-3 cups sliced brown onion
- 2 Tbsp olive oil
- ¼ cup pine nuts

One 13" Cauli Pizza Crust or one 16" Traditional Pizza Crust:

For Pesto, pulse nuts in blender or food processor until coarsely ground. Add garlic, basil, salt, olive oil and lemon juice. Blend just until pesto has desired consistency. To make the sauce, stir into a 2-qt saucepan the 2 Tbsp oil, flour, garlic powder and 3 Tbsp of the milk. Turn heat on to medium-low. Stirring constantly, add a little milk. Each time the sauce begins to thicken, add a little more until all, including the coconut milk, is used. Remove from heat. Whisk in the ¾ tsp salt and the pesto from the blender. Cover and set aside.

Preheat oven to 400°. As crust bakes the initial 45 minutes for Cauli Crust or 12 minutes for Traditional Crust, cook the onion in the oil in a large skillet over medium-low heat 25-30 minutes, stirring occasionally till caramelized.

After baking 12 minutes for Traditional Crust or 45 minutes for Cauli Crust, spread the sauce over the crust. Sprinkle chicken, artichokes, olives, onions and pine nuts on top. Bake another 8 minutes or until heated through.

Cauli Pizza Crust

Makes one 9" or one 13" Crust   Also Veg, **Grain Free**

9 Inch Crust:

- 4 cups cauliflower "rice," (approximately one 2 lb head cauliflower)
- 1½ cups water
- 1 large egg, whisked
- ⅛ tsp xanthan gum
- ¼ tsp dried oregano
- ½ tsp dried basil
- ½ tsp sea salt
- 1 clove garlic, pressed, or 1 tsp garlic powder
- parchment paper
- a clean, thin kitchen towel

13 Inch Crust:

- 12 cups cauliflower "rice," (approximately three 2 lb heads cauliflower)
- 5 cups water
- 3 large eggs, whisked
- ¼ tsp xanthan gum
- ¾ tsp dried oregano
- 1½ tsp dried basil
- 1½ tsp sea salt
- 3 cloves garlic, pressed, or 1 Tbsp garlic powder
- parchment paper
- a clean, thin kitchen towel

Grate or use a food processor to make cauliflower "rice" from the cauliflower florets. In a 4-qt pot (for a 9" crust) or a 6-qt pot (for a 13" crust), bring water to a boil. Stir in the cauliflower rice and return to a boil. Lower heat to medium, cover and cook 5 minutes. Drain using a wire mesh strainer, pressing as much water out as possible with the back of a bowl. Next, turn out onto the towel. Wrap the rice in the towel and twist, wring and squeeze tightly to remove all excess water. Take time to do this well, because it is the secret to making the slices hold together beautifully like traditional pizza. Preheat oven to 400°. Stir rice and remaining crust ingredients together in a mixing bowl. The mixture will be fluffy, light and wet. Line a pizza pan or baking sheet with parchment paper. Form crust by pressing dough about ⅓" thick and 10" wide (for a 9" crust) or 14" wide (for a 13" crust). Bake 45 minutes till golden brown. Remove from oven, spread with your choice of toppings, and return to 400° oven for another 8 minutes, or till heated through.

Traditional Pizza Crust

Makes One 16" Crust   Also Veg, V, Egg Free

- 1 cup garbanzo bean flour
- ¾ cup tapioca flour
- ½ cup arrowroot flour
- ¼ cup brown rice flour
- 1 tsp aluminum-free, GF baking powder
- 1 tsp baking soda
- 1¼ tsp sea salt
- ½ tsp dried basil leaves
- ¾ tsp garlic powder
- 1 tsp xanthan gum
- ¾ cup + 2 Tbsp warm water
- 3 Tbsp olive oil
- 2 16" lengths of wax or parchment paper, or better, one 16" length, wide enough to cover pizza pan

Preheat oven to 400°. Spray a 16" pizza pan with grapeseed oil. Also spray 1 side of the wax or parchment paper. In a large bowl, using a whisk, slowly stir all dry ingredients. Add olive oil and water. Mix well. Form a ball in the middle of the pan. Cover dough with prepared parchment or wax paper to keep it from sticking to the rolling pin. Roll the dough to the edges of the pan, then remove paper. Bake on bottom rack of oven 12 minutes until center is firm to the touch. Add your choice of sauce and toppings. Continue baking approximately 12 minutes, until edges are golden, or longer for a crispier crust.

BBQ Chicken Pizza

Serves 6   Also **Grain Free** (w/ Cauli Crust), **Egg Free** (w/ Traditional Crust)

Pizza:

1	13" Cauli Pizza Crust, or Traditional Pizza Crust, p.43
¾-1	cup Naturally Sweetened BBQ Sauce, + 3 Tbsp to toss with chicken
1½	cups chopped BBQ'd chicken or plain cooked chicken
1	cup thinly sliced red onion (about ½ a small red onion)
½	cup fresh cilantro leaves
½-1	cup Cashew Cheese, p.129, optional

BBQ Sauce   Makes 3 Cups (24 oz):

2	6 oz cans natural, unsweetened tomato paste
1	small clove garlic, pressed, or ½ tsp garlic powder
1	Tbsp apple cider vinegar
¼	cup + 1 Tbsp blackstrap molasses
⅔	cup coconut palm sugar
1	Tbsp olive oil
1⅓	cups water, or more for desired thickness
1½	tsp sea salt
1⁄16-⅛	tsp cayenne pepper, or to taste
¼	tsp GF hickory seasoning liquid smoke, such as Wright's®

Sauce:

In a 3-qt saucepan, combine all ingredients using a whisk. Simmer 10 minutes, stirring often. Pour into a 26 oz jar. Store extra BBQ sauce in refrigerator for up to 1 month.

Pizza:

Preheat oven to 400º. After baking pizza crust the initial 45 minutes for Cauli Crust or 12 minutes for Traditional Crust, spread the BBQ sauce up to ¾" from the edge. Toss the chicken in the 3 Tbsp BBQ sauce and scatter the chicken and onion over the pizza. Bake 8 minutes for Cauli Crust or 12 minutes for Traditional Crust, or until heated thru. Sprinkle with the cilantro and garnish with a dollop of Cashew Cheese if using.

This, the Creamy Pesto Pizza & the Margarita Pizza on the Cauli Crust have got to be my most favorite, sensationally fun-to-eat recipes in the book! Both because they are absolutely scrumptious & because the ingredients are shockingly clean & guilt-free. The experience goes like this...you pick up your slice of pizza & it holds together just like regular pizza. You sink your teeth into flavor galore & you could swear that you must be indulging in foods which are "no-no's" on the "off limits" list. But, in reality, you are eating cauliflower, eggs, chicken (in this recipe) and cashews. Wow!

Margarita Pizza

Makes one 13" Pizza   Also Veg, **Grain Free** (w/ Cauli Crust), V, Egg Free (w/ Traditional Crust)

1	13" Cauli Pizza Crust or Traditional Pizza Crust, p.43
1-1½	cups Tomato Free Marinara or Old World Tomato Basil Marinara, p.47
1½	cups Cashew Cheese, p.129, at room temperature
8	or more fresh whole basil leaves

Preheat oven to 400°. After baking pizza crust the initial 45 minutes for Cauli Crust or 12 minutes for Traditional Crust, spread the marinara up to ¾" from the edge. Bake another 6-8 minutes for Cauli Crust or 12 minutes for Traditional Crust, and remove from oven. Using a large spoon, drop and swirl mounds of Cashew Cheese on top of the pizza, making them 2-3" wide and ¼" thick as in photograph. Arrange the basil leaves as desired and serve.

It's time for a pizza party for those of us who not only don't eat gluten or grain, but also for those who avoid **tomatoes/nightshades**. Wow, pizza is back!

46

Tomato Free Marinara

Partial Recipe for Pizza (Makes 1½ cups)

- 1 Tbsp olive oil
- 3 large cloves minced garlic
- ¾+ lb butternut squash, to equal ¾ lb once it is peeled and seeded, cut into 1"-1½" chunks. (should measure out to be roughly 2¼ cups)
- ⅓ cup red beets, peeled, cut into 1" chunks
- ⅔ cup water
- ¾ tsp dried basil
- ¼ tsp fennel seeds
- ½+⅛ tsp sea salt
- 4 tsp fresh lemon juice
- ¼ tsp onion powder

Full Recipe (Makes 3 cups)

- 2 Tbsp olive oil
- 6 large cloves minced garlic
- 1½+ lb butternut squash, to equal 1½ lb once it is peeled and seeded, cut into 1"-1½" chunks. (should measure out to be roughly 4¼ cups)
- ⅔ cup red beets, peeled, cut into 1" chunks
- 1⅓ cups water
- 1½ tsp dried basil
- ½ tsp fennel seeds
- 1¼ tsp sea salt
- 2½-3 Tbsp lemon juice
- ½ tsp onion powder

In a 2-qt pot, stir and cook the garlic in the oil on low heat for 2 minutes. Add the water, squash and beets. It is important not to add any more than ⅓ cup beets (⅔ cup for Full Recipe), otherwise your marinara will turn bright pink. Stir in the basil and fennel, and bring it to a boil. Lower heat to simmer, cover and cook 45-50 minutes until squash and beets are very tender. Add a little water only if needed. Remove from heat and cool slightly. Transfer vegetables, including water, to a blender and add the salt, lemon and onion powder. Because of the pressure of blending hot liquids, **cover the top of the blender with a dish towel and hold lid in place** while blending until smooth. If sauce is too thick, add a little more water. Pour over your favorite GF pasta, chicken, pizza or veggies.

Old World Tomato Basil Marinara

Partial Recipe for Pizza (Makes 1½ cups)

- 1 Tbsp olive oil
- 1 clove garlic, pressed
- 1 6 oz can tomato puree
- ⅓ lb fresh Roma tomatoes, chopped, or 6-8 oz can crushed or diced tomatoes, drained
- ¼ tsp fennel seeds
- 1 Tbsp fresh basil leaves, chopped, or ⅓ tsp dried
- ¼ tsp dried oregano
- 2 tsp fresh chopped Italian flat leaf parsley
- ⅛ tsp sea salt, to taste

Full Recipe (Makes 7 cups)

- 3 Tbsp olive oil
- 3-4 cloves garlic, pressed
- 1 28 oz can tomato puree
- 1¾ lb fresh Roma tomatoes, chopped, or 28 oz can crushed or diced tomatoes, drained
- 1 tsp fennel seeds
- ¼ cup fresh basil leaves, chopped, or 1½ tsp dried
- 1 tsp dried oregano
- 3 Tbsp fresh chopped Italian flat leaf parsley
- ¼-½ tsp sea salt, to taste

For pizza sauce, use a 2-qt saucepan, or for full recipe, use a 4-qt pot. Cook the garlic in the olive oil on medium-low heat for 2 minutes. Add the tomato puree and fresh or canned tomatoes. Stir in the fennel, basil, oregano, parsley and salt. Simmer uncovered for 20 minutes, stirring occasionally.

Pasta & Rice Alternatives

Some people are finding that a grain-free diet works best for them. Others just want to "change it up," get away from the carbs in grains and enhance their diets with more vegetables and leafy greens. Yet so many favorite dishes are saucy, like pasta dishes, curries and korma. They need a "base" of something neutral to provide that beloved component of sauce-laden deliciousness. Here are several alternatives to pasta and rice which are win-wins because not only are they naturally grain free, they also add much needed phytonutrients and anti-oxidants, aid in neutralizing pH, and are anti-inflammatory. If that weren't enough, they also are lower in fat, carbohydrates, cholesterol and calories while being low glycemic and high in fiber. Here are some of the veggie "bases" that can be substituted for pasta or rice in any recipe.

- Kale & Onions, *Delightfully Free* p.107
- Beet greens, shredded cabbage or spinach, sauteed in olive oil with garlic and sea salt
- Garlic Mashed Cauli, p.124
- Squashes cut in strip or cut using a veggie pasta maker, p.49
- Spaghetti squash, p.49
- Spaghetti Squash Kale Duo, p.49
- Cauli "White Rice", p.121
- Cauli Pizza Crust, p.43

In addition to this, choices of pastas sold in markets and online have evolved to include 100% grain free versions, made from better ingredients. Gluten free pastas are now available made from quinoa, lentils, beans of all types, and buckwheat.

48

Spaghetti Squash

Makes 4½-5 Cup.   Also Veg, V, **Grain Free**, Egg Free

1	3 lb spaghetti squash (4½-5 cup "spaghetti")
1	cup water
2	cloves minced garlic, optional
2½	Tbsp olive oil, optional
¾-1	tsp sea salt, optional
1½	Tbsp minced fresh parsley or other herbs, optional

Preheat oven to 375°. Cut squash in half lengthwise. Scoop out seeds. Place cut sides down into a 9x13 baking dish with1cup water. Bake 30-35 minutes, just until tender when pierced with a knife. Cool squash and then use a fork to rake across squash and remove the strands of "spaghetti." Use spaghetti as it is in "pasta" dishes, soup and casseroles.

If more flavor is desired, heat the olive oil in a skillet over medium-low heat. Add the garlic and herbs, stirring 2 minutes. Add the "spaghetti" and the salt. Toss and heat, then serve with your favorite sauce.

Spaghetti Squash Kale Duo

Serves 4   Also Veg, V, **Grain Free**, Egg Free

5	cups water
6	cups finely shredded green kale
3	cups "spaghetti" from a 2 lb spaghetti squash
2	cloves garlic, pressed or ¾ tsp garlic powder
2½	Tbsp olive oil
1	tsp sea salt

Preheat oven to 375°. Cut squash in half lengthwise. Scoop out seeds. Place cut sides down into a 9x13 baking dish with 1 cup water. Bake 30-35 minutes, just till tender when pierced with a knife. Meanwhile, in a 4-qt pot, bring water to a boil, stir in the kale, & return to a boil. Cover, turn down heat, and cook 8 minutes. Drain water using a mesh strainer. Use a fork to rake across the cooled squash removing strands of "spaghetti." Cook the garlic (if using cloves) in olive oil in a large skillet on low heat, stirring for 1 minute. Add 3 cup "spaghetti," drained kale, salt (and garlic powder if using). Stir over medium heat just till heated through. Serve with your favorite sauce.

Cauli "White Rice"

Makes 8 servings   Also Veg, V, **Grain Free**, Egg Free

2	lb cauliflower (1 large head) makes 5-6 cups raw "rice"
2	Tbsp olive oil
1	tsp sea salt

To make the cauliflower resemble rice, grate the florets using a cheese grater, or use an electric vegetable grater which can be purchased from a kitchen store, or use a food processor to pulse until the cauliflower resembles rice.

For 6 cups cooked "White Rice": In a skillet, stir and cook the grated cauliflower in the 2 Tbsp oil and salt over medium heat for 5-6 minutes, covered when not stirring. Serve immediately, or refrigerate and use in your favorite dishes that call for white rice.

Curly Zucchini "Pasta"

Use a veggie pasta cutter, available at kitchen stores, to create different shapes & sizes of "noodles" from squashes & other vegetables. Cook in boiling water only briefly or saute in a skillet with olive oil, garlic, and sea salt.

Breads & Muffins

Olive Rosemary Bread

Makes One 9" Loaf   Also Veg, **Grain Free** (w/o brown rice flour*)

4	large eggs
2½	cups cannellini beans (approximately 1½ 15 oz cans)
4½	Tbsp grapeseed oil
3	Tbsp tapioca flour
3	Tbsp arrowroot flour
3	Tbsp brown rice flour
1½	Tbsp aluminum-free, GF baking powder
1½	tsp baking soda
1½	tsp sea salt
¼	tsp garlic powder
¼	cup coconut palm sugar
2	Tbsp minced fresh rosemary leaves
2	Tbsp + 1 tsp dehydrated minced onion
⅓	cup chopped kalamata olives
•	parchment paper

Moist, light bread to die for, with the classic flavors of savory kalamata olives & rosemary. Absolutely delicious & made from surprisingly wholesome, nutritious ingredients, the main ones being beans & eggs. All but grain free, other than 3 Tbsp of brown rice flour.* A perfect pairing with any of the pasta dishes, the Chicken in Tomato "Cream" with Olives, p.25, Italian Meatballs with Kale & Wine Sauce, p.21, and Creamy Lemon Chicken, p.25, just to name a few.

Preheat oven to 350º. Brush a 9" loaf pan with grapeseed oil and line the bottom with parchment paper. Brush the parchment paper with a little oil. If using a high-speed blender, use **medium** speed. For a standard blender, use high speed. Into the blender, put the eggs and blend 10 seconds. Add the beans and blend 30 seconds. Add the remaining ingredients except for the rosemary, onion and olives, and blend 1 minute, scraping sides of blender as needed. Stir in the rosemary, onion and olives. Pour into the pan and bake 44 minutes or until the top is firm and slightly springy and a toothpick comes out clean. Cool on a rack 15 minutes, then run a knife around the edges and turn bread out to finish cooling on the rack.

* Eliminating the brown rice flour makes the bread even moister (a little less bready). Increase bake time by 3-5 minutes & test for doneness as directed.

Buttery Spread

Makes ¼ Cup   Also Veg, Grain Free, Egg Free

¼	cup ghee, softened
1½	Tbsp olive oil
¼	tsp sea salt

In a small bowl, stir all 3 ingredients together. Cover and refrigerate. The spread will soften when sitting out of refrigerator and will firm up when it is put back in.

Classic American Bread

Makes One 9" Loaf   **Also Veg**

½ cup arrowroot flour
¼ cup brown rice flour
1 cup tapioca flour
⅓ cup sorghum flour
1 tsp baking soda
2 tsp aluminum-free, GF baking powder
1 tsp sea salt
½ tsp ground cardamom
1 tsp xanthan gum
2 large eggs
¼ cup grapeseed oil
3 Tbsp coconut palm sugar
1 cup water

Tired of dry dense GF bread? Try mine!

Optional Toppings:
3 Tbsp pumpkin seeds
2 Tbsp chia seeds
2 Tbsp sesame seeds
3 Tbsp dehydrated minced onion

One Tbsp of chia seeds alone has 2,282 mg omega 3, 752 mg omega 6, 5g fiber, 3g protein, and no sugar. The pumpkin & sesame seeds are similar in their nutritional content.

Preheat oven to 325°. Brush a loaf pan with grapeseed oil. In a large bowl, carefully stir the 4 flours, baking soda, baking powder, salt, cardamom and xanthan gum together using a wire whisk. Move slowly because the flours are very light and can puff right out of the bowl. Lift and separate the flour mixture by allowing it to pour through the whisk. In another bowl, whisk the eggs. Whisk in the oil, sugar and water until the sugar is dissolved. Stir the wet ingredients into the dry ingredients using the whisk. **Rest the batter for 10 minutes.** Spoon into the loaf pan and spread it to the edges. Tap the pan on the counter a couple of times to release any air bubbles. If using seeds or onion, sprinkle them over the top and gently pat them down with fingers. Bake 15 minutes, and rotate pan 180 degrees. Continue baking 20 minutes more (totaling 35 minutes), or until a toothpick inserted in the center comes out clean. Cool on a rack 15 minutes. Carefully turn out of the pan, slice and enjoy!

Moist, light and tender, this bread is delicious and versatile. Use it for sandwiches or toast it for breakfast. Vary the taste by adding other ingredients. For example, add 1½-2 tsp dried dill weed and 1½ Tbsp dehydrated, minced onion to the dough, Yum! -or- chop the pumpkin seeds and stir them into the dough with 1-2 tsp fresh thyme or rosemary or basil/oregano. Mince fresh onion very finely and add 2 Tbsp. For a sweeter bread, replace the seeds with walnuts or pecans. Increase the coconut sugar to ½ cup. Add 1½ tsp cinnamon and ⅓ cup raisins or unsweetened cranberries or cherries. Have fun!

Fruit & Nut Naan

Makes Three 6" Naans   Also Veg, V, **Grain Free**, Egg Free

¾ cup almond **flour**
¼ cup tapioca flour
1½ tsp coconut flour
¼ tsp sea salt
¾ cup **whole** coconut milk
1½ Tbsp chopped pistachios
1½ Tbsp chopped cashews
1½ Tbsp chopped apricots

1½ Tbsp chopped medjool or zahidi dates
1½ Tbsp chopped, unsweetened, unsulphured dried cherries
     such as Trader Joe's®
1½ Tbsp unsweetened coconut, optional
• coconut oil

I love these naans! They are fantastic with curry or korma, but also stand on their own. You could actually eat them as dessert.

In a small to medium-size bowl, whisk the flours and salt together till evenly combined. Add the milk and whisk till smooth. Stir in the nuts and fruit. Preheat a nonstick pan, or if using a pan without a nonstick surface, rub the pan with a tiny bit of coconut oil and wipe away any extra. For best results, preheat the pan 2-3 minutes on medium-high heat, then turn heat down to medium-low. Pour ⅓ of the batter into the pan. It should sizzle a little at first. Help spread the batter using the back of a spoon to make the naan approximately 6" in diameter and only ¼" thick. Cook 1½-2 minutes, check underneath with a spatula and flip it when the underneath side has browned in spots. Cook the 2nd side another 1½-2 minutes till it has browned in spots. Remove to a plate.

Naan or Garlic Naan

Makes Three 6" Naans   Also Veg, V, **Grain Free**, Egg Free

Naan:
¾ cup almond **flour**
¼ cup tapioca flour
1½ tsp coconut flour
¼ tsp sea salt
¾ cup **whole** coconut milk
• coconut oil

Garlic Naan:
¾ cup almond **flour**
¼ cup tapioca flour
1½ tsp coconut flour
½ tsp sea salt
¾ cup **whole** coconut milk
1½ Tbsp minced parsley
¼ cup finely chopped garlic
2 Tbsp finely minced white onion
• coconut oil

They are amazing! So delicious, surprisingly nutritious & so much fun! This recipe makes 2 large naans, 3 medium-size or 6 small.

*With each of these naan recipes, please note that they call for almond **flour** which is blanched & is a finer consistency than almond meal.*

In a small to medium-size bowl, whisk the flours and salt together till evenly combined. Add the milk and whisk till smooth. For Garlic Naan, stir in the parsley, garlic and onion. Preheat a nonstick pan, or if using a pan without a nonstick surface, rub the pan with a tiny bit of coconut oil and wipe away any extra. For best results, preheat the pan 2-3 minutes on medium-high heat, then turn heat down to medium. Pour ⅓ of the batter into the pan. It should sizzle a little at first. Help spread the batter using the back of a spoon to make the naan approximately 6" in diameter and only ⅛"-¼" thick. Cook 1½-2 minutes, check underneath with a spatula and flip it when the underneath side has browned in spots. Cook the 2nd side another 1½-2 minutes till it has browned in spots. Remove to a plate.

Double Chocolate Zucchini Loaf

Makes One 9" Loaf or 4 Mini Loaves   Also Veg, **Grain Free**

2 large eggs	1 tsp baking soda
¼ cup grapeseed oil	¾ tsp sea salt
1 cup + 2 Tbsp coconut palm sugar	¾ tsp xanthan gum
1¼ tsp liquid stevia	½ cup DF dark chocolate chips, optional, p.5
2 tsp vanilla	¾ cup chopped walnuts, optional
3 cups grated zucchini	
2¾ cups almond meal	
½ cup arrowroot flour	
2 Tbsp coconut flour	
⅔ cup unsweetened cocoa powder	
2 tsp aluminum-free GF baking powder	

Decadently chocolate, like eating a zucchini brownie. Even though it is chocolaty, moist & scrumptious, this bread is packed with nutrition. It can also be made as muffins with a shortened baking time of about 20 minutes.

Preheat oven to 350°. Brush pan(s) with grapeseed oil. Line the bottom(s) with parchment paper. In medium bowl, whisk eggs, oil, sugar, stevia & vanilla. Stir in zucchini. In a large bowl, whisk remaining dry ingredients except for chocolate chips & nuts. Stir wet ingredients into dry ingredients. Stir in all but 3 Tbsp of chocolate chips & nuts, if using. Rest 5 minutes. Fill pan(s) & sprinkle with remaining chocolate chips & nuts. Bake the 9" loaf 42-44 minutes (mini loaves 30 minutes) or till a toothpick comes out clean. Cool 15 minutes, run a knife around edges & turn out on rack to finish cooling. Be careful not to touch chocolate chips, because they won't be hardened yet.

Carrot Spice Bread

Makes One 9" Loaf   Also Veg, **Grain Free**

3 large eggs	2 tsp ground cinnamon
1 15 oz can cannellini beans, rinsed and drained on a paper towel	1 tsp ground ginger
	¼ tsp ground cloves
3 Tbsp grapeseed oil	1½ tsp vanilla
1⅛ tsp liquid stevia	½ tsp xanthan gum
1 cup coconut palm sugar	1¼ cups grated carrots (about 2 medium carrots)
¾ cup + 2 Tbsp almond meal	¾ cup chopped walnuts or pumpkin seeds + 2 Tbsp for top, optional
¼ cup arrowroot flour	
1 tsp sea salt	⅓ cup golden raisins, optional
2 tsp aluminum-free, GF baking powder	• parchment paper
1 tsp baking soda	

Brush a 9" loaf pan with grapeseed oil. Line pan with parchment paper. Preheat oven to 325°. For a high-speed blender, use **medium** speed. For a standard blender, use high speed. Blend eggs 20 seconds. Add beans, oil, stevia and sugar, & blend till smooth. Add remaining ingredients except carrots, nuts & raisins. Blend 2 minutes, scraping sides of blender as needed. Stir in carrots, nuts & raisins, if using. Pour into pan & sprinkle with extra nuts. Bake 1 hour or till a toothpick comes out clean. Cool on a rack 10 minutes, loosen edges with a knife & cool completely.

Seriously, this carrot bread made from beans, eggs & almond meal is fabulous. Just as moist, tender & wonderful as any out there, but chock-full of nutrition beyond just the carrots.

Lemon Poppy Seed Bread

Makes One 9" Loaf   Also Veg, **Grain Free** (w/o brown rice flour*)

- 4   large eggs
- 2⅓   cups cannellini beans (approx. 1 ½ 15 oz cans), rinsed well & drained on a paper towel
- ¼   cup grapeseed oil
- 3   Tbsp tapioca flour
- 3   Tbsp arrowroot flour
- 3   Tbsp brown rice flour
- 1½   Tbsp aluminum-free, GF baking powder
- 1½   tsp baking soda
- ¼   tsp sea salt
- 1   cup coconut palm sugar

- 1½   tsp liquid stevia
- 1½   Tbsp organic lemon extract
- 2   Tbsp fresh lemon juice
- 2   Tbsp lemon zest
- 3   Tbsp poppy seeds

This is one of my favorites because it is so moist & tastes just like the wonderful lemon poppy seed bread I remember (in my former life). But, here the ingredients are Delightfully healthy, so I enjoy eating it and feel great in more ways than one.

Preheat oven to 350º. Brush a 9" loaf pan with grapeseed oil and line the bottom with parchment paper. Brush parchment paper with a little oil. If using a high-speed blender, use **medium** speed. For a standard blender, use high speed. Into the blender, put the eggs and blend 10 seconds. Add the beans and blend 1 minute. Add the remaining ingredients except for lemon zest and poppy seeds, and blend 1 minute, scraping sides of blender as needed. Add lemon zest and poppy seeds, and blend on low 10 seconds. Pour into pan and bake 38-40 minutes or until top is firm and slightly springy and a toothpick comes out clean. Cool on a rack 15 minutes, then run a knife around edges and turn out to finish cooling on rack. When cooled completely, frost with Orange Icing if desired.

* Eliminating the brown rice flour makes the bread moister (a little less bready). Increase bake time by 3-5 minutes & test for doneness as directed.

Orange Icing

Makes 1¾ Cups   Also Veg, V, Grain Free, Egg Free

- 1½   cups raw, unsalted cashews
- ½   cup unsweetened rice or almond milk
- ½   tsp agar powder
- ¼   cup fresh orange juice

- ¼   cup raw honey
- ⅛   tsp sea salt
- ⅛   tsp liquid stevia
- ¼   tsp organic orange extract

Soak the cashews in 2 cups water for at least 2 hours if your blender is powerful, or longer (4-8 hours) for a less powerful blender. This will cause the nuts to soften and blend into a creamier texture. Rinse the nuts using a wire mesh strainer and drain well on a paper towel.

In a 1-qt pan, whisk the agar into the milk. Bring to a boil over medium-low heat, stirring with whisk 5 minutes. Remove from heat. Into a **high-speed blender,** put all ingredients and milk-agar mixture. Blend on high 1-2 minutes till smooth, scraping sides of blender as needed. The icing will continue to thicken over the next hour, even at room temperature. Use to ice cakes, breads and muffins. Store remaining icing in refrigerator.

Similar to traditional orange or lemon icing, this one is sweet, citrusy & delicious, but very smooth & a little softer. It holds its texture even when not refrigerated. Traditional icings are basically just a little citrus juice mixed with a lot of white confectioner's sugar. Consider the difference here in sugar vs. nutrition.

Savory Garden Muffins

Makes 9 Muffins   Also Veg, **Grain Free**

¾   cup finely chopped leeks
2   large cloves garlic, pressed
1   Tbsp olive oil
2   large eggs
1¼ cups roasted pureed butternut squash (home cooked or canned)
¼   tsp ground sage
1¼ tsp dried thyme, rubbed and crumbled between fingers
⅛   tsp ground nutmeg

1¼ tsp sea salt
⅓   cup grated zucchini
⅔   cup grated carrot
½   cup chopped fresh spinach
2   Tbsp minced parsley, optional
2¾ cups almond meal
2   tsp aluminum-free, GF baking powder
1½ tsp baking soda

This is a delicious change. The goodness of garden vegetables, brimming with vitamins & phytonutrients disguised as savory, warm, grain-free muffins. Brilliant!

Preheat oven to 350°. Brush a muffin tin with grapeseed oil and lay 1¼" squares of parchment paper in bottom of each muffin cup, or use paper liners. In a skillet, cook the leeks and garlic in the oil for only 2 minutes on medium-low heat until limp. Remove from heat. In a large bowl, whisk the eggs. Whisk in the squash, sage, thyme, nutmeg and salt. Stir in the zucchini, carrots, spinach, leeks and garlic from the skillet, and parsley if using. Add the almond meal, baking powder and baking soda, and stir till combined. Fill the muffin cups to the top and bake 32 minutes, or until a toothpick comes out clean. Cool on a rack 5 minutes before using a knife to loosen the edge of each muffin.

Lemon Orange Cranberry Muffins

Makes 11-12 Muffins

Also Veg, **Grain Free** (w/o brown rice flour*)

- 4 large eggs
- 2⅓ cups cannellini beans, rinsed and drained on a paper towel
- ¼ cup grapeseed oil
- 3 Tbsp tapioca flour
- 3 Tbsp arrowroot flour
- 3 Tbsp brown rice flour
- 1½ Tbsp baking powder
- 1½ tsp baking soda
- ¼ tsp sea salt
- 1 cup coconut palm sugar
- 1½ tsp liquid stevia
- 2 Tbsp fresh lemon juice
- 1 tsp organic orange extract
- 3 Tbsp orange zest
- ⅔ cup naturally sweetened dried cranberries
- • parchment paper
- 2 Tbsp finely grated orange peel, optional

Preheat oven to 350º. Brush a muffin tin with grapeseed oil and lay a 1¼" square of parchment paper in each muffin cup, or use paper liners. If using a high-speed blender, use **medium** speed. For a standard blender, use high speed. Blend eggs 10 seconds. Add beans & blend 1 minute. Add remaining ingredients except orange zest & cranberries, & blend 1 minute, scraping sides of blender as needed. Add orange zest & blend on low 10 seconds. Stir in cranberries and fill muffin cups almost full. Sprinkle with grated orange peel if desired. Bake 19-20 minutes or till tops are firm & slightly springy & a toothpick comes out clean. Cool on rack 10 minutes, run a knife around edges & turn out to finish cooling.

*Eliminating the brown rice flour makes the muffins even moister (a little less cakey). Increase bake time by 3-5 minutes & test for doneness as directed.

Sweet & citrusy, cakey & tender! Lemon Orange Cranberry Muffins might seem like a less healthy indulgence, but check the ingredients: whole, nutritious protein & fiber-rich foods.

Zucchini Muffins

Makes 12 Muffins or 35-40 Mini Muffins

Also Veg

- 2 large eggs
- 3½ Tbsp grapeseed oil
- ⅔ cup coconut palm sugar
- 1 tsp liquid stevia
- 2 tsp vanilla
- 3 cups grated zucchini
- 2¾ cups almond meal
- ½ cup arrowroot flour
- 2 Tbsp coconut flour
- 3 Tbsp brown rice flour
- 2 tsp baking powder
- 1 tsp baking soda
- ¾ tsp sea salt
- 2½ tsp ground cinnamon
- ¼ tsp ground cloves
- 1 cup chopped walnuts, divided, optional

Preheat oven to 350º. Brush muffin tin with grapeseed oil or use paper liners. In a medium bowl, whisk eggs, oil, sugar, stevia & vanilla. Stir in zucchini. In a large bowl, whisk remaining dry ingredients except for nuts. Stir wet ingredients into dry ingredients. Stir in most of nuts, if using. Rest 4 minutes. Fill muffin cups almost full. Sprinkle with remaining nuts. Bake 18 minutes or till centers of muffins are firm and a toothpick comes out clean. Cool on rack 5 minutes before loosening edges with a knife. Turn out to finish cooling.

Wonderfully moist & delicious as any muffin from the best bakery. On a nutritional note, the 2 predominant ingredients are Delightfully healthy...zucchini & almond meal. The other ingredients are also healthy, the sugar unrefined, low glycemic & minimal.

Apple Almond Quinoa Muffins

Makes 14 Muffins   Also Veg, **Grain Free**

2	cups almond meal	4	large eggs
2	cups quinoa flakes	¾	cup coconut palm sugar
½	cup arrowroot flour	¾	tsp liquid stevia
1	Tbsp ground cinnamon	⅓	cup + 1 Tbsp grapeseed oil
¼	tsp ground cloves	⅓	cup unsweetened apple sauce
1¼	tsp sea salt	1½	tsp vanilla
1	tsp baking soda	3	cups apples, cored, peeled and chopped
1	Tbsp aluminum-free, GF baking powder	½	cup chopped almonds or walnuts, optional
¾	tsp xanthan gum		

Preheat oven to 350º. Brush a muffin tin with grapeseed oil or use paper liners. In a large bowl, whisk the first 9 dry ingredients together. In a medium bowl, whisk the eggs. Whisk in the sugar, stevia, oil, apple sauce and vanilla. Stir the wet ingredients into the dry ingredients. Add the apple and nuts, if using, and stir just until combined. Rest batter 5 minutes. Fill muffin cups generously to the top. Bake 20 minutes or till a toothpick comes out clean. Cool 5 minutes in tin before using a knife around edges and removing muffins to a wire rack.

> Mouth-watering, moist muffins for breakfast, a healthy snack or a treat in lunchboxes. Proof that all kinds of wholesome, good nutrition can come in the form of a yummy muffin.

Pumpkin Muffins

Makes 10 Muffins   Also Veg, **Grain Free**

2	eggs	2¾	cups almond meal
2	cups pumpkin	⅓	cup coconut flour
2	Tbsp pumpkin spice	½	cup chopped walnuts
⅛	tsp ground cloves		
½	tsp sea salt		
⅔	cup coconut palm sugar		
2	tsp vanilla		
½	tsp liquid stevia		
1	tsp aluminum-free, GF baking powder		
½	tsp baking soda		

> These warm, velvety pumpkin muffins fill the house with the scent of cinnamon & cloves as they fill your heart with joy. Partly because they are so scrumptious, but also because each grain-free muffin contains an amazing 13½g protein, 11½g fiber with only 8g fat & 13g of unrefined, natural sugar.

Preheat oven to 350º. Brush muffin tin lightly with grapeseed oil. In a large bowl, whisk the eggs. Whisk in the remaining ingredients except for the almond meal, coconut flour and nuts. Add the almond meal and coconut flour, stirring with a large spoon. Fill muffin cups almost full and sprinkle with nuts if using. Bake 30-32 minutes or until tops of muffins are firm and a toothpick comes out clean.

Breakfasts

Traditional Grain-Free Waffles

Makes 6 Belgian Waffles   Veg, Grain Free

- 3   large eggs
- 1   15 oz can cannellini beans, rinsed with a strainer and drained on a paper towel
- ¾   tsp sea salt
- 1   tsp aluminum-free, GF baking powder
- ¼   cup arrowroot flour
- 10   drops liquid stevia
- 1   Tbsp coconut palm sugar
- •   grapeseed oil for waffle iron

Traditional taste & texture, but using very untraditional ingredients, it's magical. Just like my pancakes, these waffles reheat beautifully in the toaster. So any leftovers are a bonus for another morning when you could use a quick & easy breakfast that is amazingly nutritious!

If using a high-speed blender, use **medium** speed. For a standard blender, use high speed. Blend the eggs briefly. Add the beans and blend until smooth, scraping sides of blender as need. Add the remaining ingredients and blend 1 minute.

Brush a waffle iron generously with grapeseed oil and heat it up. Pour batter from the blender onto the waffle iron to cover about ⅔ of the bottom. The batter will spread out when iron is closed. Close iron and allow to cook several minutes. Each waffle iron is different, so check to see when waffle becomes golden. Re-oil the waffle iron if needed after cooking a few waffles.

Naturally Sweetened Berry Syrup

Makes 1¾ cups   Also Veg, V, Grain Free, Egg Free

- 1½   cups fresh or frozen (thawed) combination of strawberries, blueberries and raspberries
- 3-4 Tbsp unsweetened apple juice or water
- ¼   tsp liquid stevia
- 2   Tbsp coconut nectar, or to taste

Into a blender put all ingredients and blend until smooth. Store in refrigerator.

Faux Bisquick® Pancakes

Makes 11 pancakes   Also Veg, Grain Free

- 3   large eggs
- 1   15 oz can cannellini beans, rinsed with a strainer
       and drained on a paper towel
- ⅛   tsp sea salt
- 1   tsp aluminum-free, GF baking powder
- ¾   tsp baking soda
- ¼   cup arrowroot flour
- 1½   Tbsp coconut palm sugar
- •   grapeseed oil

If using a high-speed blender, use **medium** speed. For a standard blender, use high speed. Blend the eggs briefly. Add the beans and blend until smooth, scraping sides of blender as needed. Add the remaining ingredients and blend 1 minute.

Brush a griddle or skillet with grapeseed oil and pre-heat it. Turn heat down to medium-low. Pour batter from the blender onto griddle to make 4" pancakes. When bubbles form, check the underside of each pancake with a spatula. When underside is golden, they are ready to be flipped. Cook the second side until golden and remove to a plate. Re-oil the griddle as needed and adjust to a lower heat if needed.

OK, this is amazing! Talk about re-creating an all-time favorite & going from junky, bad-for-you ingredients to squeaky clean ones! As your family gobbles up these light, fluffy pancakes, you will smile to yourself & know that besides the fact that they are not eating stuffy, starchy, processed, refined, white wheat flour & sugar, they are enjoying 14g protein & 6g fiber for every 3 pancakes made from real, whole foods. Reheat any leftover pancakes in the toaster. They also freeze well, so make a double batch to have a healthy, hot breakfast ready to go on other busy mornings.

69

"Cream Cheese" 🍹

Makes 2½ Cups   Also Veg, Grain Free, Egg Free

2	cups raw, unsalted cashews
2	Tbsp water
3	Tbsp fresh lemon juice
1¼	tsp sea salt
1	Tbsp ghee, softened
2	tsp white vinegar

Unbelievable! We could have called this "I Can't Believe it's Not Cream Cheese" because you will think it is. My husband says it's better! This is perfect for bagels, tea sandwiches, as a spread for hors d'oeuvres, a topping for fruit desserts, anything you would spread with cream cheese. The possibilities are endless!

Soak the cashews in 2 cups of water for at least 2 hours if your blender is powerful, or longer (4-8 hours) for a less powerful blender. This will cause the nuts to soften and blend into a creamier texture. Rinse the nuts using a wire mesh strainer and drain well on a paper towel. Into a **high-speed** blender, put the nuts and all of the remaining ingredients. Blend on high 1-2 minutes until the consistency is very smooth and creamy. Use a silicone spatula to scrape down the sides of the blender as needed. Transfer the mixture to a 3-4 cup container with a lid and refrigerate. The "Cream Cheese" will firm up in 4-5 hours and will be firmer still after being chilled 8-10 hours. Store in the refrigerator for up to 3 weeks.

Natural Berry Jam

Makes about 2 Cups   Also Veg, V, Grain Free, Egg Free

1	lb strawberries, blueberries, raspberries, blackberries, peaches or plums
2-4	Tbsp raw honey, if desired based on sweetness of the fruit
15-20	drops liquid stevia, if desired based on sweetness of the fruit
2	Tbsp chia seeds

If using strawberries, peaches or plums, remove pits, stems and/or leaves, and chop them. In a 2-qt pan, stir and mash the fruit with a masher or large fork as it cooks over medium heat for 5 minutes. Bring to a boil, stir and cook another 5 minutes. Remove from heat and stir in the honey and stevia as needed depending on the sweetness of the fruit. Stir in the chia seeds and cook 1 minute at a low boil. Remove from heat, stir and allow to thicken about 10 minutes as it cools. If it seems too thin, add another 1-2 tsp chia seeds, but remember that it will continue to thicken as it chills. Store in refrigerator for up to 2 weeks.

Think of Natural Berry Jam on your bagel or toast as adding important nutrients needed for good health. Chia seeds are high in omega 3s. They're also way-high in fiber, so much so, that they absorb 10 times their weight & size in any liquid they're mixed with. Mix them with fresh, juicy berries & together they become an unprocessed, naturally sweetened jam that is wonderfully high in omega 3s & fiber, & at the same time, very low glycemic. Not to mention that berries are one of our best sources of antioxidants & for reducing inflammation. Fabulous!

Cinnamon Breakfast Strudel

Serves 8   Also Veg

6	9" GF, corn-free tortillas, such as Trader Joe's® or Food for Life®	1	Tbsp ground cinnamon
1½	tsp olive oil (¼ tsp for each tortilla. An oil mister is recommended)	¾	tsp sea salt
		½	cup coconut palm sugar
8	large eggs	½	tsp stevia
⅔	cup **light** coconut milk	4½	cups thinly sliced apple
1	tsp ground cloves	¾	cup chopped walnuts, optional

Spray a 10" pie dish and both sides of each tortilla very lightly with an oil mister. Use a pastry brush to spread oil evenly. Preheat oven to 350°. In a large bowl, whisk eggs, milk, spices, sugar and stevia. Soak each tortilla in egg mixture 1 minute as you use it, coating edges too. Lay first tortilla in bottom of pie dish and pour approximately ⅙ of egg mixture over tortilla. Use pastry brush to spread egg mixture evenly over tortilla. Lay ⅕ of apple and sprinkle with ⅙ of nuts. Repeat with remaining 5 tortillas and egg mixture, ending with the last of egg mixture covering the top tortilla and sprinkle with nuts. All of apple is used between tortilla layers. Bake 35-40 minutes. Cool on a rack 8 minutes, slice and serve.

This pretty egg/pastry dish looks like you worked hours to make it & have your degree from culinary school, but it is actually simple to make. Your family & friends will ask for it again & again.

Garden Breakfast Pie

Serves 8   Also Veg

6	9" GF, corn-free tortillas, such as Trader Joe's® or Food for Life®	1½	tsp sea salt
1½	tsp olive oil (¼ tsp for each tortilla. An oil mister is recommended)	⅓	tsp white pepper
		½	tsp ground coriander
1¼	cups white onion	½	tsp ground nutmeg
1½	Tbsp + ½ Tbsp grapeseed oil		
2	cups chopped broccoli		
6	large eggs		
¾	cup **light** coconut milk		

Flakey pastry-like layers filled with savory, creamy broccoli & onion. Picture perfect for that special breakfast, but so easy to prepare, it makes breakfast on any ordinary day extraordinary.

Spray a 10" pie dish and both sides of each tortilla very lightly with an oil mister. Use a pastry brush to spread oil evenly. Preheat oven to 350°. In a skillet, cook onion in 1½ Tbsp oil, stirring occasionally 4 minutes on medium-high heat. Add ½ Tbsp oil and broccoli. Cook 4 minutes, stirring occasionally. Remove from heat.

In a large bowl, whisk the eggs, milk and seasonings. Stir in the onions and broccoli from skillet. Lay the first tortilla in the bottom of the pie dish and pour approximately ⅙ of the egg-broccoli mixture over the tortilla. Use the pastry brush to spread the egg mixture over all of the tortilla. Repeat with the remaining 5 tortillas and egg-broccoli mixture, ending with the last of the egg-broccoli mixture covering the top tortilla. Bake 35 minutes. Remove from oven and allow to set 8 minutes before serving.

Artichoke & Herb Egg Casserole

Serves 5-6   Also Veg, Grain Free

2½   cups canned artichoke hearts, in water (not marinated)
      drained, **OR** Brussels sprouts, sliced ¼" thick

1¼   cups thinly sliced red onion

1½   Tbsp olive oil

¾   cup **light** coconut milk

½   of one 15 oz can garbanzo beans (almost 1 cup),
      rinsed and drained well

2   large cloves garlic or 1¾ tsp garlic powder

1¼   tsp sea salt

1½   tsp Herbs de Provence

1   Tbsp coconut flour

8   large eggs

Either with artichokes or with Brussels sprouts, this fluffy, savory dish will be a new breakfast or brunch favorite!

Preheat oven to 400º. For the artichoke casserole, in a 9x13 baking dish toss onion in the 1½ Tbsp oil till coated. Or for the Brussels sprouts casserole, in a 9x13 baking dish toss Brussels sprouts and the onion in the 1½ Tbsp oil till coated. Roast in the oven 10 minutes, just till slightly tender. Remove from oven and set aside. Adjust oven heat to 325º. Brush a 7x11 baking dish or 4 to 5, 8-10 oz ramekins generously with grapeseed oil. Into a blender pour the milk, beans and garlic. Blend on high 20 seconds (or, if using a high-speed blender, use **medium** speed) until smooth. Add salt, Herbs de Provence, flour and eggs, and blend 40 seconds (on medium if using a high-speed blender). Pour into the baking dish or ramekins. Scatter the artichokes, **or** the Brussels sprouts, and the onion evenly over top. Bake casserole 35 minutes or the ramekins 20-25 minutes.

Tomato Basil Quiche

Serves 8   Also Veg

1	cup thinly sliced leeks
1¼	cups thinly sliced crimini mushrooms
1½	Tbsp olive oil
1	large clove garlic pressed or 1 tsp garlic powder
5	large eggs
⅓	cup **light** coconut milk
½	cup finely minced fresh basil
1⅛	tsp sea salt
⅓	tsp black pepper
1½	cups chopped tomatoes, drained of juice
1	9" Pie Crust: Savory Nut Crust, as in photo, or
	Basic Pie Crust, p.157

In a skillet, cook the leeks and mushrooms in the oil over medium-low heat 4 minutes. Stir in the garlic and cook 1 more minute. Remove from heat and set aside. In a large bowl, whisk the eggs. Whisk in the milk, basil, salt and pepper. Stir in the tomatoes and the leeks and mushrooms from the skillet. Pour into crust and bake 35 minutes or until the center of the quiche is firm. Cool on a rack 10 minutes and serve.

The luscious flavor of herbs, mushrooms & tomatoes in a "buttery" crust with a light crunch that melts in your mouth. This quiche reminds me of those favorite breakfast spots that usually have a patio of potted flowers and fabulous food--which--we can't eat because of all the gluten, dairy, sugar...Now, enjoy that same kind of fare, made clean & healthy, in your own home with family & friends. Try it in the Savory Nut Crust as in the photo, or in the Basic Pie Crust.

Breakfast Cookies

Makes 14 Cookies   Also Veg, **Grain Free**

2 eggs
¾ cup almond butter
½ cup coconut palm sugar
½ tsp liquid stevia
2 tsp vanilla
¼ cup unsweetened apple sauce
½ tsp sea salt
½ tsp baking soda
1 tsp aluminum-free, GF baking powder
1¼ cups almond meal
¼ cup coconut flour
¾ cup apple, peeled, cored and finely chopped
¾ cup coarsely chopped almonds, optional
2 Tbsp raw sunflower seeds, optional

Cookies for breakfast?! These breakfast cookies look & taste like a departure from healthy eating, but not so. They are grain free & consist of almonds, sunflower seeds, apples & coconut with a relatively small amount of low-glycemic, unrefined coconut palm sugar—just under 3½ tsp for 2 cookies.

Other Optional Additions:
1 Tbsp chia seeds
¼ cup raisins or chopped dates or dried cranberries
⅓ cup unsweetened coconut

Perfect for breakfast on the run!

Preheat oven to 350º. Brush a baking sheet generously with grapeseed oil. In a large bowl, whisk the eggs. Stir in the almond butter, sugar, stevia, vanilla, apple sauce, salt, baking soda, baking powder, almond meal and coconut flour till well combined. Fold in the apples, almonds, sunflower seeds and optional ingredients if using any. Drop 2 Tbsp-size mounds of dough onto baking sheet and bake 13-14 minutes. Cool 3 minutes on a rack, remove with spatula and enjoy. Reheat on another morning for 2-3 minutes.

Bacon Buckwheat Biscuits

Makes 12

4	oz turkey bacon, chopped into ½" pieces	1⅓	cup brown rice flour
1	cup chopped brown onion	¾	cup uncooked cream of buckwheat cereal,
1	Tbsp olive oil		such as Bob's Red Mill® or Pocono®
2	large eggs	2½	Tbsp coconut palm sugar
¼	cup grapeseed oil	1	tsp sea salt
¼	cup unsweetened rice or almond milk	½	tsp baking soda
4	oz can mild or hot diced green chiles,	2	tsp aluminum-free, GF baking powder
	very well drained	½	tsp xanthan gum

In a skillet, cook the bacon and onion in the 1 Tbsp olive oil on medium heat, stirring often for 6-7 minutes. Remove from heat and set aside. Preheat oven to 350º. Brush a baking sheet with grapeseed oil. In a medium bowl, whisk the eggs. Whisk in the oil, milk and chiles. In a large bowl, whisk the remaining dry ingredients. Pour the egg mixture into the dry ingredients. Stir in the bacon and onion until combined. Drop 2½" mounds onto baking sheet and press down gently with fingers. Bake 14 minutes. Cool 3-4 minutes. Remove with a spatula. Refrigerate any uneaten biscuits.

Here is a breakfast of eggs, buckwheat & bacon rolled into a country biscuit..or two... hard to stop there because the flavor of bacon with onion & chiles is so good.

Cinnamon Crunch Oat-Free Granola

Makes 7 Cups   Also Veg, V, Grain Free, Egg Free

½	cup almond meal	¾	cup coconut palm sugar
¼	cup **whole** buckwheat groats such as Arrowhead Mills® or Pocono® brand	2	Tbsp ground cinnamon
⅓	cup quinoa flakes such as Ancient Harvest® brand	½	tsp ground ginger
1	cup chopped walnuts	¼	tsp + ⅛ tsp sea salt
1	cup sliced almonds		
¼	cup raw sunflower seeds		
1	Tbsp sesame seeds		
⅓	cup unsweetened coconut, optional		
¼	cup + 2 Tbsp water		

Crispy, crunchy, sweet, wholesome & even grain free! This granola is more than just a yummy treat. It's packed with nutrition, fiber & protein plus the wonderful flavor and anti-inflammatory benefits of cinnamon & ginger.

Preheat oven to 350º. Brush a rimmed baking sheet generously with grapeseed oil or use parchment paper. In a large bowl, mix the first 8 ingredients. In a 1-qt saucepan, stir the sugar into the water and bring to a boil over medium-low heat, stirring often. Cook 30 seconds more after it boils and remove from heat. Stir in the cinnamon, ginger and salt. Pour over the dry ingredients and mix thoroughly. Spread out evenly and not too thickly on the baking sheet and bake 18 minutes. Cool 15 minutes and then loosen with a spatula before allowing it to finish cooling. It will continue to crisp up as it cools.

Spiced Breakfast Bake

Serves 6-8   Also Veg, Grain Free (w/o Topping)

To double recipe see note below

4   large eggs

1   15 oz can white beans such as cannellini, navy or Great Northern, rinsed in a strainer and drained on a paper towel

3   Tbsp arrowroot flour

1   Tbsp almond meal

¼   tsp sea salt

1½   tsp aluminum-free, GF baking powder

1   tsp baking soda

1½   Tbsp ground cinnamon

¾   tsp ground ginger

½   tsp ground cloves

2   tsp vanilla

¾   tsp + ⅛ tsp liquid stevia

¼   cup + 2 Tbsp coconut palm sugar

Crumble Topping:

2   Tbsp coconut oil, softened

¼   cup almond meal

2   Tbsp brown rice flour

⅛   tsp liquid stevia

2½   Tbsp coconut palm sugar

½   tsp ground cinnamon

¼   tsp ground cloves

•   pinch of sea salt

2   Tbsp uncooked creamy buckwheat cereal*, such as Bob's Red Mill® or Pocono®

2   Tbsp whole buckwheat groats

⅓   cup coarsely chopped walnuts, pecans or almonds, optional

*If your buckwheat groats are not toasted (still a greenish-tan color), toast them by spreading on a rimmed baking sheet and bake only 6 minutes at 350°.

For Crumble Topping: In a mixing bowl, stir together everything but the buckwheat and nuts, using the back of a spoon until the texture is even. Stir in the buckwheat, and nuts if using.

Preheat oven to 350°. Brush an 8x8 pan with grapeseed oil. If using a high-speed blender, use **medium** speed. For a standard blender, use high speed. Blend the eggs 20 seconds. Add the beans and blend till smooth. Add the remaining ingredients except for the Crumble Topping and the nuts. Blend until well combined. Pour into pan, sprinkle with nuts or the Crumble Topping if using, or both. Bake 18-20 minutes or until top is firm (20-22 minutes if using Crumble Topping.) Enjoy warm or cool completely. Refrigerate if storing for more than 1 day.

Having a brunch or breakfast party? Double the recipe & bake it in a 9x13 pan for 22 minutes or 25 minutes if using the Crumble Topping. No one will believe that this fabulous, cakey "indulgence" is actually made out of eggs, beans & natural sweeteners. Check the ingredients again & note how clean & pure they are.

SOUPS

SMOKEY BEAN SOUP

Serves 6-8   Also Veg & V (w/ Vegetable Broth), Egg Free

1	cup chopped onion
1	Tbsp olive oil
64	oz chicken stock or broth
2	cups cooked lima beans or one 15 oz can, rinsed and drained
2	cups cooked black-eyed peas or one 15 oz can, rinsed and drained
½	cup uncooked millet
10-12	leaves of beet greens or more, 2½ cups, stems removed, sliced 1"
⅛	tsp GF liquid smoke, such as Wrights®
¾-1	tsp moderately hot, fire-roasted chipotle powder
1	small clove minced garlic, or ¼ tsp garlic powder
1½	tsp sea salt

Prepare beet greens and set aside. In a 6-qt pot, cook the onion in the oil 6 minutes on medium-low, covered when not stirring. Pour in the chicken stock, lima beans, peas and millet, and bring to a boil. Lower heat to medium and cook at a gentle boil 10 minutes. Add the beet greens and cook covered another 10 minutes. Turn off the heat and stir in the liquid smoke and seasonings. Serve immediately or reheat to serve later.

Sure to be a new favorite, this is a satisfying soup with a warm, lightly smokey, mildly chipotle flavor. I love the texture of the beet greens. They're a little like pasta & a clever way to get high doses of calcium, magnesium, lutein & beta-carotene.

Pumpkin Ginger Soup

Serves 5-6   Also Veg & V (sub vegetable broth), Grain Free, Egg Free

1½	Tbsp olive oil	¾	tsp ground cinnamon
2	tsp ghee	½	tsp ground ginger, or more to taste
1	cup chopped yellow onion	1	tsp sea salt
1	small clove minced garlic or	2	Tbsp coconut palm sugar
	½ tsp garlic powder	⅓	cup chopped apple, optional garnish
4	cups (32 oz) chicken stock or broth	3	Tbsp chopped walnuts or pumpkin seeds,
3½	cups pureed pumpkin or one 29 oz can		optional garnish

In a skillet, cook the onion in the oil and ghee over medium-low heat 8 minutes, covered when not stirring. Add the fresh garlic, cook 2 more minutes and remove from heat.

Into a blender, pour 2 cups of the chicken stock, the pumpkin and the onion-garlic from skillet. Blend till smooth. Into a 4-qt pot, pour the puree from blender, the remaining chicken stock, the seasonings and the sugar. Because the consistency of pumpkin varies, you may need to add 2-6 Tbsp water. Stir over medium-low heat 10 minutes, covered when not stirring. Serve topped with chopped apple and seeds or nuts if desired.

Festive, warm & inviting, Pumpkin Ginger Soup
makes a delicious, memorable meal.

Asparagus & Leek Bisque

Serves 8   Also Veg & V*, Grain Free, Egg Free

2	Tbsp ghee (*sub olive oil)
1	cup thinly sliced leeks
4	cups chicken stock or broth (*sub vegetable broth)
4	cups cauliflower, (about ½ of a 2 lb head), cut in 1½"-2" chunks
2½	lb asparagus, ends removed, cut in 1" lengths
1¼	tsp sea salt
¼	tsp white pepper
2	tsp sherry, optional

Creamy, smooth and delicious. This elegant soup is made of 2 nutritiously potent vegetables, asparagus & cauliflower which fight cancer and inflammation, and are great sources for vitamins A, B, C, E & K as well as being rich in folate which improves brain function and supports fetal development.

Cut and measure all ingredients. In a 6-qt pot, melt the ghee over low heat. Add the leeks and cook 5 minutes, covered when not stirring. Add the chicken stock and bring to a boil. Add the cauliflower and return to boil. Cover, turn heat down slightly to a low boil and cook 2 minutes. Stir in the asparagus, cover and cook 8 minutes more. Remove from heat. Allow soup to cool 10 minutes.

Reserve 1 cup of asparagus tips in a small bowl. Transfer soup to a blender half at a time and blend till smooth. If using a high-speed blender, use **medium** speed. Transfer back to the 6-qt pot, stir in the salt, pepper and reserved asparagus tips. Stir over medium heat till heated through.

Like Cream of Potato Soup

Serves 6   Also Veg (w/o bacon), Grain Free, Egg Free

1	medium brown onion, chopped (about 2 cups)
1½	Tbsp olive oil
2	tsp ghee
6	cloves garlic, pressed
1½	Tbsp minced fresh parsley
1	cup finely sliced, then chopped green kale
2½	cups unsweetened rice or almond milk
2	15 oz cans garbanzo beans, rinsed and drained on a paper towel
½	cup water
1¾	tsp sea salt
¾	tsp black pepper
¼	lb turkey bacon, chopped, scrambled in a pan with 1 Tbsp olive oil, optional
⅓	cup sliced black olives
⅓	cup sliced green onion

Creamy, yet made without any cream or potatoes! White potatoes are composed of simple carbs which break down quickly, convert to sugar, spike our blood glucose level and are stored as fat. The garbanzo beans in this soup are complex carbs, high in protein & fiber (helping to stabilize blood sugar), & are very low in sugar & fat.

In a skillet, cook the onion in the olive oil and ghee 6 minutes, covered when not stirring. Add the garlic and parsley, and cook 2 minutes as you stir. Remove from heat, reserve 1 cup of the onion-garlic in a small bowl and set aside. In a 1-qt pot, bring the kale and ¾ cup water to a boil. Cover, reduce heat and cook 5 minutes. Drain the water and set aside. Into a blender, pour the milk, beans and onion-garlic from the skillet. Blend until smooth. Transfer to a 4-qt pot and stir in the reserved 1 cup onion-garlic, the kale, ½ cup water, salt, pepper and bacon, if using. Cook 20 minutes on medium-low heat, stirring often, covered when not stirring. Serve sprinkled with olives and green onions.

Tex Mex Soup

Serves 6   Also Veg, V, Grain Free, Egg Free

1	medium chopped brown onion
1½	Tbsp olive oil
3	cloves minced garlic
4	cups water
1	15 oz can black beans, rinsed and drained
¾	cup pinto beans, rinsed and drained
1¾	cups chopped Roma tomatoes or one 15 oz can tomatoes, drained
3	Tbsp tomato paste
1	cup cooked spaghetti squash, p.49
2¾	tsp sea salt
½	tsp chipotle powder
2½	tsp chili powder
2	tsp cumin
2	Tbsp fresh lime juice
⅓	cup packed fresh cilantro leaves
½	cup sliced black olives + extra for garnish
1	medium avocado, diced

In a 6-qt pot, cook onion in oil 5 minutes on low heat. Add garlic, cook and stir 2 minutes. Add water, both beans, tomatoes, tomato paste, spaghetti squash and seasonings. Bring to a boil, lower heat to simmer, cover and cook 10 minutes. Stir in lime juice, cilantro and olives, cover and cook 2 minutes. Serve topped with avocado and olives.

Savory, spicy & satisfying, this Southwest soup is quick to make & has a fabulous array of nutritious ingredients, including plenty of protein if you eat vegetarian/vegan, or not. For those who miss the chicken, add 1 cup cooked chicken, 4 cups chicken stock instead of the water and reduce the salt to taste.

BUTTERNUT VEGETABLE SOUP

Serves 8   Also Veg, V (sub vegetable broth), Grain Free, Egg Free

1 medium brown onion, chopped (2-2½ cups)	1½ Tbsp minced fresh sage or 1¾ tsp ground
1½ Tbsp olive oil	32 oz (4 cups) chicken stock or broth
2 cups + 2½ cups raw butternut squash, seeded, peeled & cubed ½"	2 cups chopped broccoli
2 large cloves minced garlic	¾ cup chopped red bell pepper
1 Tbsp fresh thyme leaves or ¾ tsp dried	1 tsp sea salt

In a large skillet, cook the onion in the oil 3 minutes over medium-low heat, covered when not stirring. Add the 2 cups squash, garlic and herbs, and cook 9 minutes. Remove from heat. In a 4-qt pot, bring 2 cups of the broth to a boil. Add the 2½ cups squash, cover and cook 4 minutes. Stir in the broccoli and red pepper, cover and cook 5 minutes, just till bright green and tender crisp. Meanwhile, into a blender pour the remaining 2 cups of the broth and the onion-squash from the skillet. Blend till smooth. Pour the onion-squash from the blender into the pot with the squash-broccoli-red pepper. Add the salt, heat on medium low and serve.

So pretty & so good! A tasty new combo of vegetables & herbs in a wonderful creamy broth.

CREAMY LENTIL SOUP

Serves 4   Also Veg, V, Grain Free, Egg Free

1 cup dry green lentils	1 cup unsweetened rice or almond milk
2 Tbsp olive oil	1 Tbsp fresh lemon juice
2 cups chopped brown onion	½ tsp cumin
⅔ cup sliced carrot	1¾ tsp sea salt
2 large cloves minced garlic	1½ cups finely chopped tomatoes, optional
2 cups water	

In a 2-qt pan, bring 2 cups water to a boil, stir in the lentils and cook on medium heat 15 minutes or until water is absorbed. Reserve ¾ cup of the lentils to a small bowl and set both aside. Meanwhile, in a skillet, cook the onion and carrot in the olive oil on medium heat 10 minutes until soft, covered when not stirring. Stir in the garlic and cook 2 more minutes. Remove from heat.

Into a blender, pour the 2 cups water and the onion-carrot from the skillet and blend until smooth. Add the lentils from the pan and blend again till creamy. Pour soup from blender into a 4-qt pot. Stir in the milk, seasonings, the reserved lentils and tomatoes, if using. Cook over medium heat just until heated through and serve.

Hearty and so tasty, Creamy Lentil Soup is a great alternative source of protein. Lentils are rich in protein, fiber, folate and iron, and are low in calories with virtually no fat. And even though this lentil soup tastes creamy, it is dairy free.

CREAM OF CHICKEN SOUP

Serves 8   Also Veg & V (sub vegetable broth), Grain Free, Egg Free

- 5   cups cauliflower, cut in 2" chunks
- 1   medium brown onion, chopped (2-2½ cups)
- 1½   Tbsp olive oil
- 2   large cloves garlic, pressed
- 1½   tsp fresh thyme leaves or ¾ tsp dried
- 1   Tbsp minced fresh sage or ½ tsp ground
- 32   oz (4 cups) chicken stock or broth, divided
- ¾-1   tsp sea salt
- 2   cups chopped cooked chicken

Creamy with savory herbs & chicken, this soup is satisfying, quick & easy to whip up, yet very clean, healthy & nutritious. It checks all "the boxes" including that it saves time because it makes enough for 2 dinners for most families.

In a 3-qt pot, bring 3 cups water to a boil, add the cauliflower, return to a boil, cover, lower heat and cook 10 minutes till very soft. Drain all water.

In a skillet, cook the onion in the oil over medium heat 7 minutes. Add the garlic and herbs (if using fresh), stir and cook 2 minutes. Remove from heat.

Into a blender, pour 2 cups of the broth, the drained cauliflower and onion-garlic-herbs from the skillet. Blend till smooth. Transfer to a 4-qt pot and add the remaining 2 cups of the broth, herbs (if using dried), salt and chicken. Stir over medium heat till hot and serve.

ITALIAN SAUSAGE & CABBAGE SOUP

Serves 4   Also Grain Free, Egg Free

- ½   lb uncooked sweet Italian chicken sausage, casings removed
- 1   Tbsp olive oil
- 32   oz chicken stock or broth
- 2   tsp fennel seed
- 3   cups sliced green cabbage
- 1   cup white beans, such as navy or cannellini
- ½   tsp sea salt

Sausage & Cabbage Soup is the perfect dinner on a chilly night when you don't have much time, but do want much flavor. Cabbage is one of the top 10 "superfoods."

In a skillet, scramble the sausage in the oil over medium heat 10 minutes, stirring often, covered when not stirring. Drain and set aside.

In a 4-qt pot, bring the chicken broth and fennel seed to a boil. Add the remaining ingredients including the sausage and bring back to a boil. Cover, reduce heat to medium-low and cook 10 minutes, stirring occasionally.

Salads

Balsamic Pear & Pomegranate Salad with Cashew "Cheese"

Makes 4 Entree Salads or 8-10 Sides

Also Veg & V (w/o Chicken), Grain Free, Egg & Vinegar Free

- 2-3 cups sliced red d'Anjou or other pear (2-3 pears)
- ½-¾ cup pomegranate seeds
- 1 cup halved raw walnuts
- ½ cup sliced green onions
- 5 oz arugula (6 cups)
- 1 cup Cashew Cheese, p.129
- • Vinegar Free Balsamic Dressing or Balsamic Vinaigrette, see recipe below
- 8 oz grilled chicken or fish, optional

Add the optional chicken or fish and serve it with the Zucchini Muffins, p.63 or the Apple Almond Quinoa Muffins, p.65, & you have a lovely ladies' luncheon. May I suggest the Chocolate "Cheesecake", p.155 or Raspberry "Cheesecake", p.153, for dessert?

Arrange the pear, pomegranate seeds, walnuts & green onions on a bed of arugula on each plate. Top each with chicken or fish, if using, the dressing and a dollop of Cashew Cheese. Or, toss all ingredients except the Cashew Cheese and then top each salad with a dollop of Cashew Cheese.

Balsamic Vinaigrette Dressing:

- ½ cup red wine vinegar
- ½ cup balsamic vinegar
- 1 cup grapeseed oil
- ¼ tsp sea salt
- 1½ Tbsp coconut palm sugar
- 1 small clove garlic, pressed, or ¼ tsp garlic powder
- ½ tsp ground mustard
- ¼ cup water
- • pinch paprika
- ¼ tsp + ⅛ tsp xanthan gum
- 8 drops liquid stevia, optional

Pour all ingredients, except xanthan gum, into a jar with a tight-fitting lid and shake well. Add xanthan gum and shake again. For smoother flavors, emulsify the dressing by mixing all ingredients, except xanthan gum, in a blender on high 30 seconds. Add xanthan gum and blend again 10 seconds. Store in refrigerator.

Vinegar-Free "Balsamic Vinaigrette":

- ¾ cup 100% unsweetened cranberry juice, such as Trader Joe's® brand
- 1 cup grapeseed, sunflower or rice bran oil
- ½ cup fresh lemon juice
- 3 Tbsp coconut palm sugar, or more to taste
- 1⅛ tsp sea salt
- 1½ tsp prepared horseradish (not creamy)
- 1¾ tsp ground mustard
- 1 small clove garlic, pressed, or ½ tsp + ⅛ tsp garlic powder
- • pinch paprika
- 16 drops liquid stevia
- ¼ tsp + ⅛ tsp xanthan gum

Shake all ingredients, except the xanthan gum, together in a jar with a tight-fitting lid. Add the xanthan gum and shake again. For smoother flavors, emulsify the dressing by mixing all the ingredients, except xanthan gum, in a blender 30 seconds. Add xanthan gum and blend again 10 seconds. Store in the refrigerator.

GOLDEN BEET & KALE SALAD

Makes 3-4 Entree Salads or 8-10 Sides   Also Veg, V, Grain Free, Egg Free, Vinegar Free

- 1¼ lb golden beets (about 4 medium)
- 3 cups shredded, moderately packed green kale
- ½ cup grated carrot
- ½ cup sliced green onion

- ¼ cup sunflower seeds
- ½ cup cooked white quinoa
- ¼ cup minced parsley
- • Lemon Dill Dressing

Can be made a day ahead.

Wash, scrub and trim beets, removing tops and bottoms. In a 2 or 3-qt pot, bring 5 cups of water to a boil. Cook beets, covered for 20 minutes at a low boil. Rinse with cold water, drain and cool to room temperature. Peel and slice the beets ⅓" thick. Then halve and/or quarter them to bite-size. Beets will be tender crisp. In a large bowl, toss the beets and the remaining ingredients, including the amount of Lemon Dill Dressing desired.

Lemon Dill Dressing:
- ¼ cup olive oil
- ½ cup grapeseed, sunflower or rice bran oil
- ½ cup fresh lemon juice
- ¾ tsp sea salt
- 1 med-large clove garlic, pressed, or 1¼ tsp garlic powder
- 1 tsp dried dill weed

Pour all ingredients into a jar with a tight-fitting lid and shake well. Store in refrigerator.

This great tasting combination of deep greens, root vegetables & seeds delivers straight nutrition in the form of phytonutrients, antioxidants, anti-inflammatory components, vitamins, minerals, fiber & protein.

SUMMER BERRY SALAD

Makes 2 Entree Salads or 4-6 Sides   Also Veg, V (w/o chicken) Grain Free, Egg Free

Salad:
- 3-4 oz spring or field greens (4-5 cups)
- 1 cup fresh sliced strawberries
- ½ cup fresh raspberries
- ½ cup fresh blackberries or blueberries
- 2 large kiwis, peeled and sliced
- ⅔ cup sliced avocado
- ¼ cup sliced green onion
- ⅔ cup sliced, cooked chicken
- ⅓ cup toasted pecans
- • Summer Berry Vinaigrette
- ¼ cup Cashew Cheese, p.129, optional

Summer Berry Vinaigrette:
- ¾ cup grapeseed, sunflower or rice bran oil
- ½ cup white balsamic vinegar
- ½ cup fresh or frozen (defrosted) raspberries
- ⅛ tsp sea salt
- 5 drops liquid stevia

Pour all ingredients into a blender and blend until smooth. Store in refrigerator.

In a large bowl, toss all ingredients except for pecans and Cashew Cheese. Divide onto individual plates. Top with Cashew Cheese if using and sprinkle with pecans.

Thanksgiving Turkey Salad with Cranberry Sauce

Makes 2 Entree Salads   Also Egg Free

Salad:

- 4 cups chopped green cabbage
- 2 cups fresh spinach
- 1½ cups turkey, cut in bite-size pieces
- 1 cup sliced or cubed, unpeeled apple
- ½ avocado, cubed
- ⅓ cup coarsely chopped walnuts
- ⅓ cup Orange Cranberry Sauce, p.124
- • Cranberry Vinaigrette Dressing

In a large bowl, toss all ingredients, except for the Orange Cranberry Sauce, or toss the cabbage, spinach and turkey with some Cranberry Vinaigrette Dressing. Divide onto individual plates and top with the apple, avocado, a spoonful of Orange Cranberry Sauce, and sprinkle with the walnuts.

Cranberry Vinaigrette Dressing:

- ⅔ cup grapeseed, sunflower or rice bran oil
- ½ cup balsamic vinegar
- ¾ cup **unsweetened**, 100% cranberry juice, such as Trader Joe's®
- 1 Tbsp coconut palm sugar
- 8-10 drops liquid stevia
- ¼ tsp + ⅛ tsp xanthan gum

Blend all ingredients, except xanthan gum, 20 seconds in a blender. Add xanthan gum and blend 10 seconds. Store in refrigerator.

Turkey "Sandwich" Salad

Makes 2 Entree Salads   Also Egg Free, Vinegar Free

- 1 small head romaine lettuce, chopped
- 1½ cups turkey, cut in bite-size pieces
- ½ cup Herbed Turkey Dressing, p.125
- ¼ cup chopped brown onion
- 1 small tomato, sliced, optional
- ⅓ cup Orange Cranberry Sauce, p.124, optional
- • Creamy Mustard Dressing, p.106

Thanksgiving leftovers make this tasty twist on a salad almost as delicious as the Thanksgiving spread. All the highlights of Thanksgiving dinner, plus Creamy Mustard Salad Dressing is like eating the famous day-after Thanksgiving turkey sandwich, sans the bread.

In a small bowl, toss the turkey with 3 Tbsp of the Creamy Mustard Dressing. In a large bowl, toss the romaine, onion and tomatoes, if using, with Creamy Mustard Dressing. Place in 2 serving bowls, top with the turkey, Herbed Turkey Dressing and a dollop of Orange Cranberry Sauce, if using.

Roasted Beet & Arugula Salad

Makes 4 Entree Salads or 10-12 Sides

Also Veg, V, Grain Free, Egg Free, Vinegar Free

1¼ lb golden beets (about 4 medium)
4 oz arugula, about 5-6 cups
⅔ cup shaved fennel
1 large avocado, sliced

¼ cup pistachios
3 Tbsp pomegranate seeds
• Cashew Cheese, p.129, optional
• Light Lemon Dressing, see recipe below

Preheat oven to 400°. Wash, scrub and trim beets, removing tops & bottoms. In a covered baking dish with ½" depth of water, roast the beets, covered, 1 hour or till tender when pierced with a fork. Cool beets. Peel and slice beets in ¼" rounds.

In a large bowl, toss the arugula and fennel with Light Lemon Dressing to taste. Divide the greens onto individual plates and arrange the remaining ingredients on top, or toss all ingredients except for the Cashew Cheese. Garnish with a dollop of Cashew Cheese, if using, and serve.

Light Lemon Dressing:
1½ cups grapeseed, sunflower or rice bran oil
⅔ cup fresh lemon juice
1 tsp sea salt
1 clove garlic, pressed, or 1 tsp garlic powder

Pour all ingredients into a jar with a tight-fitting lid and shake well. Store in refrigerator.

This beautiful salad tastes as wonderful as it looks. It is sophisticated enough for a society luncheon & is at the same time packed with health-giving nutrients.

Summer Grilled Veggie Salad with Chicken

Makes 2 Entree Salads

Also Veg & V (w/o Chicken), Grain Free, Egg Free

• a bed of your favorite greens
• a combination of the grilled veggies from the Summer Grilled Chicken & Vegetables, p.27
4-6 oz grilled chicken from the same recipe, sliced
4-6 slices avocado
10 egg tomatoes, halved, optional
• Balsamic Vinaigrette, p.105

Toss all ingredients, including dressing, or assemble the ingredients atop the bed of greens and serve with the Balsamic Vinaigrette Dressing.

Salmon Mango Salad

Makes 2 Entrees　　　　　Also Grain Free, Egg Free

2	pieces wild caught salmon, totaling about ¾ lb
1	Tbsp olive oil + extra
1	cup thinly sliced red onion
1	large, ripe mango, peeled and sliced
4-6	oz baby spring greens
•	Avocado Citrus Dressing, p.104

This flavorful salad isn't just a delicious meal, it's **super food!** Salmon, mango & avocado are all on the "must-eat-for-better-health list," not to mention that the remaining ingredients, olive oil, onion & greens, are also healthful, beneficial foods.

Preheat oven to 425°. Brush a 9x7 baking dish and the salmon with olive oil. Place fish in baking dish, sprinkle with sea salt and bake uncovered 14-18 minutes depending on thickness. To determine when salmon is done, insert a fork and gently twist. As soon as it flakes, the salmon in done. Remove from oven. Meanwhile, in a skillet, cook the onion in 1 Tbsp olive oil on medium heat for only 4-5 minutes. Remove from heat. Make a bed of lettuce on each plate. Place a piece of salmon on the lettuce and pour the Avocado Citrus Dressing over. Top with the onion. Arrange the mango around the salmon and serve immediately.

Yum! Creamy & rich in taste. Avocados are considered a super food. They are rich in antioxidants which fight free radicals, are anti-inflammatory, and lower your level of bad cholesterol. In addition, 1 cup provides you with these daily values: 40% of fiber, 25% vitamin C, 20% vitamin B6, and 21% potassium. So, the deliciousness of Avocado Citrus Dressing is the bonus we get for pouring it over our salad.

Curry Ginger Chicken Salad

Makes 3-4 Entrees　　　　　Also Grain Free, Egg Free

3	cups cooked chicken cut in ½"-¾" cubes	½	cup sliced green onions
½	cup Creamy Curry Ginger Dressing, see below	¾	cup snow peas cut in 1" pieces, optional
¾	cup apple chopped in ½" pieces	½	cup whole raw cashews
1	cup red grapes, halved lengthwise, or fresh pineapple cut into ½" pieces	6-8	oz spring mix or other favorite salad greens

In a medium bowl, mix chicken with ½ cup of dressing and then stir in apple, grapes or pineapple, and green onions. Make a bed of salad greens in each bowl and spoon a mound of chicken salad on top. Add snow peas if using. Pour Curry Ginger Dressing over and top with the cashews. The chicken salad mix can be made several days ahead.

Creamy Curry Ginger Dressing:

1½	cups soy-free mayonnaise, such as Soy-Free Vegenaise®	½	tsp ground ginger
		¾	tsp sea salt
6	Tbsp unsweetened rice or almond milk	⅛	tsp cayenne pepper
1	Tbsp + 1 tsp curry powder	2	Tbsp coconut palm sugar
		6-8	drops liquid stevia

Whisk all ingredients or shake them in a jar with a tight-fitting lid. Store in refrigerator.

A delicious & pretty luncheon fare or nice summer dinner. The chicken salad mixture is also wonderful in a sandwich using the Classic American Bread, p.53.

Salad Dressings

Why make your own salad dressings? We obviously want dressings that are GF, DF and SF. You can put a "Check" in that box. These dressings are full of herbs and healthy ingredients in a wide range of flavors. But, in addition to that, consider that my dressings contain no soy, nitrates, nitrites, high fructose corn syrup, hydrolyzed corn protein, MSG, sodium benzoate or bisulfate, maltodextrin...you get the picture. I like to save bottles with nice flip-top spouts or tight-fitting lids to use for my salad dressings or BBQ sauce.

Thai "Peanut" Dressing

Makes 1 Cup   Also Veg, V, Grain Free, Egg Free, Vinegar Free, Peanut Free

- ½ cup sunflower seed butter
- 6-7 Tbsp very hot water
- 2 Tbsp + 1 tsp GF, soy-free seasoning sauce such as Coconut Secret® Coconut Aminos
- ¾ tsp sesame oil
- 5 drops liquid stevia

In a medium bowl, stir the sunflower seed butter and a couple Tbsp of the hot water at a time together until blended and smooth. Stir in the remaining ingredients. Store in a covered container in the refrigerator.

Avocado Citrus Dressing

Makes almost 2 Cups   Also Veg, V, Grain Free, Egg Free, Vinegar Free

- 1 cup ripe avocado (about 2 medium avocados)
- ½ cup fresh orange juice
- ¼ cup fresh lemon juice
- ¼ tsp sea salt
- 1 small clove garlic, pressed, or ½ tsp garlic powder
- ⅛ tsp cayenne pepper
- 1½-2½ Tbsp water, if needed

Either whisk all ingredients together in a medium bowl, or blend briefly. Store in refrigerator.

Creamy Italian Dressing

Makes 2¼ Cups   Also Veg, V, Grain Free, Egg Free

- ¼ cup + 2 Tbsp olive oil
- ⅔ cup grapeseed oil
- ½ cup soy-free mayonnaise such as Soy-Free Vegenaise®
- ¾ cup red wine vinegar
- 2 large cloves garlic, pressed, or 1¾ tsp garlic powder
- 1 tsp sea salt
- 1⅛ tsp black pepper
- 2 Tbsp fresh oregano leaves or 1 Tbsp dried
- 1/16 tsp xanthan gum

In a medium bowl, whisk all ingredients, or blend all ingredients, except xanthan gum, 30 seconds on medium speed. Add xanthan gum and blend 10 seconds. Store in refrigerator.

CRANBERRY VINAIGRETTE

Makes 2 Cups　　　　　　　　Also Veg, V, Grain Free, Egg Free

- ⅔ cup grapeseed, sunflower or rice bran oil
- ½ cup balsamic vinegar
- ¾ cup **unsweetened**, 100% cranberry juice, such as Trader Joe's®
- 1 Tbsp coconut palm sugar
- 8-10 drops liquid stevia
- ¼ tsp + ⅛ tsp xanthan gum

Blend all ingredients, except xanthan gum, 20 seconds in a blender. Add xanthan gum and blend 10 seconds. Store in refrigerator.

SUMMER BERRY VINAIGRETTE　 MAKES 1¾ CUPS　　See Recipe on p.97

BALSAMIC VINAIGRETTE

Makes 2¼ Cups　　　　　　　Also Veg, V, Grain Free, Egg Free

- ½ cup red wine vinegar
- ½ cup balsamic vinegar
- 1 cup grapeseed oil
- ¼ tsp sea salt
- 1½ Tbsp coconut palm sugar
- 1 small clove garlic, pressed, or ¼ tsp garlic powder
- ½ tsp ground mustard
- ¼ cup water
- • pinch paprika
- ¼ tsp + ⅛ tsp xanthan gum
- 8 drops liquid stevia, optional

Pour all ingredients, except xanthan gum, into a jar with a tight-fitting lid and shake well. Add xanthan gum and shake again. For smoother flavors, emulsify the dressing by mixing all ingredients, except xanthan gum, in a blender 30 seconds. Add xanthan gum and blend again 10 seconds. Store in refrigerator.

VINEGAR-FREE "BALSAMIC VINAIGRETTE"

Makes 2¼ Cups　　　　　　Also Veg, V, Grain Free, Vinegar Free, Egg Free

- ¾ cup 100% unsweetened cranberry juice, such as Trader Joe's® brand
- 1 cup grapeseed, sunflower or rice bran oil
- ½ cup fresh lemon juice
- 3 Tbsp coconut palm sugar, or more to taste
- 1⅛ tsp sea salt
- 1½ tsp prepared horseradish (not creamy)
- 1¾ tsp ground mustard
- 1 small clove garlic, pressed, or ½ tsp + ⅛ tsp garlic powder
- • pinch paprika
- 16 drops liquid stevia
- ¼ tsp + ⅛ tsp xanthan gum

Shake all ingredients, except the xanthan gum, together in a jar with a tight-fitting lid. Add the xanthan gum and shake again. For smoother flavors, emulsify the dressing by mixing all the ingredients, except xanthan gum, in a blender 30 seconds. Add xanthan gum and blend again 10 seconds. Store in the refrigerator.

Creamy Mustard Dressing

Makes 2¼ Cups   Also Veg, V & Egg Free (substitute Soy-Free Vegenaise®),
                                                          Grain Free

- 1 cup soy-free mayonnaise, such as Soy-Free Vegenaise®
- ½ cup deli-style mustard with horseradish
- ½ cup prepared mustard
- ¼ cup water

Whisk all four ingredients or shake them in a jar with a tight-fighting lid. Store in refrigerator.

Lemon Dill Dressing

Makes 1¼ cups   Also Veg, V, Grain Free, Egg Free, Vinegar Free

- ¼ cup olive oil
- ½ cup grapeseed, sunflower or rice bran oil
- ½ cup fresh lemon juice
- ¾ tsp sea salt
- 1 med-large clove garlic, pressed, or 1¼ tsp garlic powder
- 1 tsp dried dill weed

Pour all ingredients into a jar with a tight-fitting lid and shake well. Store in refrigerator.

Light Lemon Dressing

Makes just over 2 Cups   Also Veg, V, Grain Free, Egg Free, Vinegar Free

- 1½ cup grapeseed, sunflower or rice bran oil
- ⅔ cup fresh lemon juice
- 1 tsp sea salt
- 1 clove garlic, pressed, or 1 tsp garlic powder

Pour all ingredients into a jar with a tight-fitting lid and shake well. Store in refrigerator.

Creamy Green Onion Dressing

Makes 2¾ Cups   Also Veg, V, Grain Free, Egg Free, Vinegar Free

- 1 cup grapeseed, sunflower or rice bran oil
- 1 cup white beans (cannellini, navy or Great Northern), rinsed & drained on a paper towel
- 1½ cups green onions or scallions, chopped in 1" lengths, packed
- 3 Tbsp fresh lemon juice
- 2 tsp sea salt
- 1 medium clove garlic, or 1 tsp garlic powder
- 4-5 Tbsp water

Into a blender, put the oil and beans, and blend 30 seconds or till smooth. Add the remaining ingredients and blend till smooth. Store in refrigerator.

Ginger Sesame Dressing

Makes 1½ cups   Also Veg, V, Grain Free, Egg Free, Vinegar Free

- 1 cup grapeseed, sunflower or rice bran oil
- ⅓ cup fresh lemon juice
- 3 Tbsp toasted sesame oil
- 1⅓ tsp sea salt
- 2½ tsp ground ginger
- ¼ tsp + ⅛ tsp cayenne pepper
- ½ tsp ground mustard
- 1 small clove garlic, pressed, or ½ tsp garlic powder

Pour all ingredients into a jar with a tight-fitting lid and shake well. Or blend all ingredients in a blender until smooth. Store in refrigerator.

Creamy Curry Ginger Dressing

Makes 2 Cups   Also Veg, V, Grain Free, Egg Free, Vinegar Free

- 1½ cup soy-free mayonnaise, such as Soy-Free Vegenaise®
- 6 Tbsp unsweetened rice or almond milk
- 1 Tbsp + 1 tsp curry powder
- ½ tsp ground ginger
- ¾ tsp sea salt
- ⅛ tsp cayenne pepper
- 2 Tbsp coconut palm sugar
- 6-8 drops liquid stevia

Whisk all ingredients or shake them in a jar with a tight-fitting lid. Store in refrigerator.

Grapefruit White Wine Dressing

Makes 2¼ Cups   Also Veg, V, Grain Free, Egg Free, Vinegar Free

- ¼ cup olive oil
- ¾ cup grapeseed, sunflower or rice bran oil
- 1 cup fresh grapefruit juice (can substitute lemon juice)
- 3½ Tbsp white wine
- ½ tsp sea salt
- 18 or more drops liquid stevia, depending on sweetness of grapefruit
- ¼ tsp + ⅛ tsp xanthan gum

Pour all ingredients into a jar with a tight-fitting lid and shake well. Store in the refrigerator.

BBQ Sauce with Natural Sweeteners

Makes 3 Cups (24 oz)   Also Veg, V, Grain Free, Egg Free

- 2 6 oz cans natural, unsweetened tomato paste
- 1 small clove garlic, pressed, or ½ tsp garlic powder
- 1½ Tbsp apple cider vinegar
- ¼ cup + 1 Tbsp blackstrap molasses
- ⅔ cup coconut palm sugar
- 1 Tbsp olive oil
- 1⅓ cup water, or more for desired thickness
- 1½ tsp sea salt
- 1/16 -⅛ tsp cayenne pepper, or to taste
- ¼ tsp GF hickory seasoning liquid smoke, such as Wright's®

In a 3-qt saucepan, combine all ingredients using a whisk. Simmer 10 minutes, stirring often. Pour into a 26 oz jar. Store in refrigerator up to 1 month.

Vegetables & Sides

Squashes with Citrus, Basil & Walnuts

Serves 8   Also Veg, V*, Grain Free, Egg Free

- 2 Tbsp ghee (* sub olive oil)
- ½ of 1 medium red onion, cut in chunks, about 2 cups
- 1 large orange bell pepper, cut in ¼" strips, about ⅓ cup
- 3 cups summer squash, sliced ¼" thick
- 3 cups zucchini, sliced ¼" thick
- ¾ tsp sea salt
- 3 Tbsp grated orange zest
- ¾ cup lightly packed basil leaves, minced
- 1 Tbsp olive oil
- ½ cup toasted walnut halves

Tender-crisp squashes with a hint of butter & citrus, the tang of fresh basil & the light crunch of toasted walnuts. Gorgeous to serve to guests but quick & simple to make.

Cut and measure all ingredients. In a large skillet, melt the ghee over low heat. Adjust heat to medium. Add the onion. Stir and coat with ghee, cover and cook 2 minutes. Stir in the bell pepper, cover and cook 1 more minute. Add the squashes and the 1 Tbsp olive oil. Coat with the ghee/oil, cover and cook 6 minutes, just till vegetables are crisp-tender. Remove from heat, stir in the salt, orange zest and basil. Serve immediately topped with the walnuts.

Curry & Coconut Cauli Rice

Makes 4-5 Servings   Also Veg, V, Grain Free, Egg Free

- 1 cup chopped brown onion
- 1½ cups shredded green kale, moderately packed
- 3 Tbsp coconut oil, divided
- 1 large clove minced garlic or 1 tsp garlic powder
- 4 cups raw Cauli "White Rice", p.121
- ½ cup fresh or frozen peas
- 3¼-3½ tsp curry powder
- 1⅛ tsp sea salt
- ¼ tsp cumin
- 2½ Tbsp unsweetened coconut

Spice up an ordinary dinner with these 3 vegetables which masquerade as a rice dish. On top of the great flavor, these incredible vegetables are all nutrient dense, anti-inflammatory, high in anti-oxidants, good for weight management and help fight various forms of cancer.

In a skillet, cook the onion and kale in 2 Tbsp of the oil over medium heat for 6 minutes, covered when not stirring. Lower heat to low, stir in the garlic and cook 2 minutes. Add the remaining 1 Tbsp oil, turn heat up to medium and stir in the remaining ingredients. Cook another 8 minutes, stirring occasionally, covered when not stirring.

Toasted Brussels Sprouts, Yams & Beets

Serves 5-6   Also Veg, V, Grain Free, Egg Free

16   oz Brussels sprouts, halved (3-4 cups)
1   large yam, peeled and cut into 1¼" pieces (3-4 cups)
2   medium-size red beets, peeled and cut into 1" pieces (3-4 cups)
4   Tbsp olive oil, divided 1 Tbsp + 3 Tbsp
½   Tbsp + 1½ Tbsp chopped fresh rosemary
½   tsp + 1 tsp garlic powder
⅓   tsp + ½ tsp sea salt

A flavorful combination. Roasted & seasoned with garlic & rosemary, this dish can turn a "vegetable hater" into a vegetable enthusiast.

Preheat oven to 375°. Brush an 8x11 baking dish and a 9x13 baking dish lightly with olive oil. Toss the beets in a medium bowl with the 1 Tbsp oil, ½ Tbsp rosemary, ½ tsp garlic powder, and ⅓ tsp sea salt. Turn out into the 8x11 baking dish and roast 30-35 minutes, until tender when pierced with a fork.

Meanwhile, in a large bowl, toss the Brussels sprouts and yams in the 3 Tbsp oil, 1½ Tbsp rosemary, 1 tsp garlic powder, and ½ tsp sea salt until well coated. Turn out into the 9x13 baking dish and roast at 375° for 20 minutes or until tender when pierced with a fork. Remove from oven. Toss with the beets, and serve.

Toasted Kabocha Squash with Citrus Coriander "Butter"

Serves 8   Also Veg, Grain Free, Egg Free

1   small-medium kabocha squash (3-3½ lbs)
2   Tbsp coconut oil or olive oil
•   sea salt

Wash and dry the squash. For peeled squash, use a sharp vegetable peeler. Or, without peeling the squash, use a large, sharp knife to carefully cut the squash in half and then into 1" wedges. Preheat oven to 400°. Put the coconut oil in a large baking dish and place it in the oven for 1 minute to melt the oil. Remove from oven and toss the squash wedges so they are coated in oil. Sprinkle with sea salt and roast, covered for 20 minutes till tender. Serve with or without Citrus Coriander "Butter."

Roasted Kabocha Squash hits the spot on flavor & on nutrients. It's a good source of fiber, especially with its peel which becomes soft when roasted. It is rich in iron, vitamin C and certain B vitamins as well as beta-carotene used to produce vitamin A. Plus, one cup of kabocha has only 7g of carbs and only 40 calories compared to butternut squash which has 16g of carbs and 60 calories.

Citrus Coriander "Butter":

2½   Tbsp ghee, softened
2   Tbsp orange zest
1½   tsp lemon zest
1   Tbsp olive oil
¼   tsp sea salt
⅛   tsp ground coriander
2   drops liquid stevia, optional

Citrus Coriander "Butter" is wonderful on more than just kabocha squash. It adds luscious flavor to any vegetable or rice. Try it on GF toast!

In a small bowl, stir all ingredients together. Store in the refrigerator.

Brussels Sprout Fritters

Makes 10   Also Veg, Grain Free

4	cups finely chopped raw Brussels sprouts	1½	tsp sea salt
½	cup finely chopped carrots	¼	tsp xanthan gum
3	large eggs	⅓	cup almond meal
3	cloves garlic, pressed or 1½ tsp garlic powder	½	cup finely chopped brown onion
¾	tsp fresh thyme or ¼ tsp dried	•	olive oil

To chop the Brussels sprouts, place whole Brussels sprouts in a blender 1 cup at a time and pulse blender 6-8 times till Brussels sprouts are in small shreds. Remove to a bowl and repeat until all Brussels sprouts are shredded. Do the same thing with the carrots. In another medium bowl, whisk the eggs, garlic, thyme and salt. Add xanthan gum and whisk again. Stir in the almond meal, onion and vegetables.

Brush a skillet generously with olive oil and pre-heat on medium-low. Form 3" pancakes and cook about 4 minutes until golden brown on the bottom. Flip with a spatula and cook the other side another 4 minutes until golden brown. Remove from skillet and serve as a side dish or even for breakfast. Delicious with the Creamy Scallion Sauce, p.133.

Switch it up & try these for breakfast with fried eggs. Or serve them with Italian Sausage & Cabbage Soup, p.93 or Creamy Lentil Soup on page 91. They are so tasty & sort of fall into the "naughty" hash browns category, except they are made entirely of vegetables, whole food proteins & are pan "fried" with just a little healthy olive oil. Enjoy them as your main course, especially with Creamy Scallion Sauce, p.133 which adds even more phytonutrients, protein & fabulous flavor.

Southern Greens with Andouille Sausage

Makes 2 entrees or 4 sides   Also Veg, V (w/o sausage & sub vegetable broth)
                                     Grain Free, Egg Free

1	medium brown onion, sliced
1½	Tbsp olive oil
2	cloves minced garlic
1	14-15 oz can chicken stock or broth
1	tsp sea salt
¼	tsp black pepper
16	oz combination of fresh greens such as collard, beet, turnip, mustard and spinach
2	cooked andouille chicken sausages (about 6 oz), casings removed, chopped

What a scrumptious way to get your daily dose of anti-oxidants, flavonoids and pH balance from dark greens.

In a large pot, cook onion in the oil over medium heat 6 minutes. Add garlic and cook 2 more minutes. Stir in remaining ingredients. Cover and cook 8 minutes, stirring occasionally, till greens are soft, but not overcooked.

Sesame Ginger Vegetables

Makes 3 Entrees or 7-8 sides   Also Veg, V, Grain Free, Egg Free, Vinegar Free

- 1½ cups broccoli florets, cut 1"
- 1½ cups unpeeled Persian cucumber, sliced ¼" thick
- 1½ cups asparagus, cut 1½"
- 1½ cups sugar snap peas, cut 1"
- 1 cup chopped red bell pepper, cut ¾"
- 1 cup finely chopped white onion
- 4 or more leaves of Chinese cabbage
- 3 Tbsp toasted sesame seeds
- • Ginger Sesame Dressing

We need a variety of raw vegetables to boost our health. This dish delivers a knock-out punch! Together, the raw broccoli, cucumbers, asparagus, sugar peas, red bell peppers, white onion and Chinese cabbage fight inflammation, arthritis and cancer, and supply incredible doses of vitamins A, C & K, plus the B vitamins, iron and folate which improves brain function among other amazing benefits. Eating healthy has never been tastier.

In a large bowl, toss the first 6 ingredients with the Ginger Sesame Dressing, to taste. Serve on the Chinese cabbage leaves, sprinkled with the sesame seeds.

Make this into a complete meal by tossing in bite-size pieces of chicken.

Ginger Sesame Dressing (1½ cups):

- 1 cup grapeseed, sunflower or rice bran oil
- ⅓ cup fresh lemon juice
- 3 Tbsp toasted sesame oil
- 1⅓ tsp sea salt
- 2½ tsp ground ginger
- ¼ tsp + ⅛ tsp cayenne pepper
- ½ tsp ground mustard
- 1 small clove garlic, pressed, or ½ tsp garlic powder

Pour all ingredients into a jar with a tight-fitting lid and shake well. Or blend all ingredients in a blender until smooth. Store in refrigerator.

Stir Fried Baby Bok Choy

Serves 4   Also Veg, V, Grain Free, Egg Free

- 12-14 oz (about 6) baby bok choy or one 12-14 oz head
- ¾ cup thinly sliced red bell pepper
- 2 Tbsp olive oil
- 1 tsp sesame oil
- 3 cloves minced garlic
- • sea salt
- • red chili pepper flakes, optional

Cut off any remaining root base at the very bottom of each bok choy. Pull off each leaf and cut the white thicker bottom of each leaf off, then slice each of the largest leaves in half lengthwise. In a wok or skillet, cook the thicker, white lower parts of the leaves with the red bell pepper in the olive oil and the sesame oil on medium-low heat for 3 minutes. If using a skillet, cover when not stirring. Stir in the remaining green leaves and garlic, stirring constantly for 2 minutes. Remove from heat, sprinkle with sea salt and red chili pepper flakes, if using. Serve immediately.

Cauli "Potato" Salad

Makes 7½ Cups or 12 Servings Also Veg, Grain Free

- 3 lb cauliflower (1 large head), 7-8 cups
- 6 cups water
- ½ cup chopped red onion
- 6 hard boiled eggs, chopped
- ½ cup chopped kosher dill pickles
- 1¼ cups soy-free mayonnaise, such as Soy-Free Vegenaise®
- 1¾ tsp + ⅛ tsp sea salt
- ¼ tsp black pepper
- ¼ tsp garlic powder

Finally! Take a huge helping of "potato" salad and enjoy every bite as you remind yourself that even though your mouth is telling you that you are splurging big time, the truth is you're eating cauliflower!

In a 4-qt pot, bring water to a boil and add cauliflower. Return to a boil, cover, lower heat slightly, and cook 5-6 minutes, just until cauliflower feels tender but not overly soft when pierced with a fork. Drain the water and fill the pot with cold water to prevent cauliflower from cooking further. Drain water again and spread cauliflower out on a baking sheet which is covered with several layers of paper towels to drain for 30 minutes or till dry. Cut cauliflower into ¾"-1" pieces and put into a large bowl. Add the remaining ingredients and toss gently until well mixed. Refrigerate at least 8 hours or best overnight.

Russet potatoes, found in traditional potato salad, have nearly 4 times the carbs as cauliflower. On top of that, they have a high glycemic index of 76 while cauliflower comes in at...zero!! Cauliflower...lower calories, a quarter the carbs, a non-existent glycemic index, over double the fiber, and high in vitamin C...it's a no brainer!

Quinoa & Lentils with Olives

Makes 4 Entrees or 8-10 Sides   Also Veg, V, Grain Free, Egg Free

- 1 cup dry lentils
- 1 cup dry black or red quinoa, rinsed well and drained
- 1 15 oz can white beans, rinsed and drained
- 1 cup finely chopped yellow onion
- 1 cup sliced green olives
- 1¼ cups toasted, coarsely chopped walnuts
- 2½ tsp sea salt
- 3 cloves minced garlic or 2 tsp garlic powder
- 3 Tbsp fresh oregano or 1¾ tsp dried
- ⅓ cup chopped fresh parsley
- ½ cup olive oil
- ¼ cup fresh lemon juice

Make a day ahead.

In a 2-qt pot, bring 2½ cups water to a boil and add the lentils. Return to a boil, lower heat and cook 8 minutes. Remove from heat. Drain using a wire mesh strainer and rinse with cold water to keep from cooking further. Drain well. In a 2-qt pot, bring 2 cups water to a boil and add the quinoa. Return to a boil, lower heat and cook about 20 minutes, stirring occasionally till water is absorbed. Remove from heat.

In a large bowl, combine the lentils, quinoa and the remaining ingredients. Toss to mix well. Add more olive oil and lemon juice if needed. Refrigerate overnight to infuse the flavors. Serve either hot or chilled.

A tasty blend of herbs, olives & toasted nuts combined with the interesting mix of lentils & quinoa. Wonderful heated as a side dish/main dish or chilled as a salad. Abundant in nutrients, fiber & protein.

117

Broccoli, Apples & Almonds with Thai "Peanut" Dressing

Serves 6   Also Veg, V, Grain Free, Egg Free, Peanut Free

- 4 cups broccoli florets, cut ½"
- 2 cups **unpeeled** apple, cored, cut in ½" pieces
- ½ cup sliced green onions
- ½ cup jicama, cubed ½"
- ⅓ cup raw slivered almonds
- 1 tsp toasted sesame seeds
- • Thai "Peanut" Dressing, p.104

Here's a fresh take on eating broccoli. The combo of flavors and crunch is wonderful, but consider the health benefits. Not only is raw broccoli high in fiber, it's rich in vitamins A, B, C & K, as well as iron, zinc & phosphorus. It is especially high in phytonutrients which means it destroys free radicals & lowers the risk of developing diabetes, heart disease & certain cancers. Definitely a win-win!

In a large bowl, toss the first 5 ingredients with "Peanut" Asian Dressing. Sprinkle with the sesame seeds.

Lentils & Quinoa with Grapefruit & Cherries

Makes 6-8 Servings   Also Veg, V, Grain Free, Egg Free

- 1¼ cups dry green lentils
- ⅔ cup dry white quinoa
- 1 cup Grapefruit White Wine Dressing (see below)
- 2½ Tbsp grated orange zest
- ½ tsp sea salt

- ⅔ cup unsweetened, unsulphured dried cherries, such as Trader Joe's®
- ½ cup sliced green onion
- ¾ cup fresh grapefruit sections, cut 1"
- ⅔ cup toasted chopped walnuts

In a 2-qt pot, bring 3 cups of water to a boil and add the lentils. Return to a boil, lower heat to a gentle boil and cook only 8 minutes. Rinse lentils with cold water in a mesh strainer and drain. Pour into a large bowl. Rinse the quinoa well with water using the mesh strainer. Bring 1⅓ cups water to a boil in the 2-qt pot, stir in the quinoa, cover, lower heat and cook 15 minutes. Remove from heat and let stand 5 minutes covered. Add quinoa to bowl with lentils. Stir in the 1 cup dressing, orange zest and salt. Refrigerate for a couple hours or overnight if possible. When ready to serve, toss in the green onion, grapefruit and nuts.

Grapefruit White Wine Dressing:

- ¼ cup olive oil
- ¾ cup grapeseed, sunflower or rice bran oil
- 1 cup fresh grapefruit juice
- 3½ Tbsp white wine
- ½ tsp sea salt
- 18 or more drops liquid stevia, depending on sweetness of grapefruit
- ¼ tsp + ⅛ tsp xanthan gum

A nice variation for quinoa adding the light crunch of par-cooked lentils & walnuts to the sweetness of citrus & cherries. Packed with protein & fiber.

Pour all ingredients into a jar with a tight-fitting lid and shake well. Store in refrigerator.

Cauli "White Rice"

Makes 8 servings   Also Veg, V, Grain Free, Egg Free

- 2 lb cauliflower (1 large head) makes 5-6 cups raw "rice"
- 2 Tbsp olive oil
- 1 tsp sea salt

To make the cauliflower resemble rice, grate the florets using a cheese grater, or use an electric vegetable grater which can be purchased from a kitchen store, or use a food processor to pulse until the cauliflower resembles rice.

For 6 cups cooked "White Rice": In a skillet, stir and cook the grated cauliflower in the 2 Tbsp oil and salt over medium heat for 5-6 minutes, covered when not stirring. Serve immediately, or refrigerate and use in your favorite dishes that call for white rice.

Wow, wow, WOW! Anything you used to make using white rice can be revolutionized, becoming amazingly clean, healthy, fabulously **low-glycemic**, shockingly **low-calorie**, even high in **fiber, phytonutrients, anti-oxidants and anti-inflammatory!** All by switching to the surprisingly versatile vegetable, cauliflower. Cauliflower lends itself to mimicking some otherwise "off limits" foods like white rice, Curry & Coconut Cauli Rice, p.109 Indian Korma, p.17, various "rice" dishes, p.121, mashed potatoes, p.124, "Potato" Salad, p.117, even "Cauli Pizza Crust" on page 43. Stir it into soups, salads and casseroles. Also wonderful, it is so quick & easy.

Lemon Rosemary Cauli Rice

Makes 4-5 Servings   Also Veg, V, Grain Free, Egg Free

- 1 cup chopped yellow onion
- 3 Tbsp coconut oil, divided
- 1 small clove minced garlic or ½ tsp powder
- 2 tsp fresh rosemary leaves
- 2 Tbsp lemon zest
- 1½ Tbsp fresh lemon juice
- 1¼ tsp sea salt
- 4 cups **raw** Cauli "White Rice" as directed above

In a skillet, cook the onion in 2 Tbsp of the oil 6 minutes on medium heat, covered when not stirring. Lower heat and stir in the garlic and rosemary, and 1 Tbsp additional oil. Stir and cook 2 minutes. Turn heat up again to medium and stir in the lemon zest, lemon juice, salt and the raw cauli rice. Cook 8 minutes, stirring occasionally, covered when not stirring.

Curry & Coconut Cauli Rice

Makes 4-5 Servings   Also Veg, V, Grain Free, Egg Free

Recipe on p.109

Herbed Cauli Rice with Dates, Pomegranates & Pistachios
Serves 4-6   Also Veg, V, **Grain Free**, Egg Free

4	cups **raw** Cauli "White Rice", p.121
1½	Tbsp + 1½ Tbsp olive oil
¼	tsp + ⅛ tsp ground ginger
½	cup minced fresh dill
3	Tbsp fresh lemon juice
⅓	cup pomegranate seeds
6-8	large soft dates, such as medjool or zahidi, pitted and coarsely chopped
⅓	cup toasted pistachios
¾	tsp sea salt crystals

Pomegranates & Cauliflower, what a pair! They both possess strong anti-oxidant properties, fight cancer & are anti-inflammatory.

You can make this wonderful dish a day ahead.

In a skillet, cook the raw cauli rice in 1½ Tbsp of the oil 5 minutes on medium heat, covered when not stirring. Remove from heat. Stir in the remaining 1½ Tbsp oil and remaining ingredients except for the pistachios and salt. Cover and refrigerate 4 hours to overnight. To serve, stir in the pistachios and salt, and enjoy.

Citrus Black Rice with Apricots & Walnuts
Makes 10-12 sides   Also Veg, V, Egg Free

1¼	cups black rice	1	large clove minced garlic or 1¼ tsp garlic powder
1	cup dry "red" lentils	1	tsp sea salt
1	cup finely chopped brown onion	•	freshly ground black pepper
1	Tbsp + ¼ cup olive oil	1	cup dried apricots, sliced ⅓"
⅓	cup grated orange zest	½	cup sliced green onions
½	cup fresh orange juice	½	cup cilantro leaves
1½	Tbsp fresh lemon juice	⅔	cup chopped walnuts

In a 4-qt pot, bring 2½ cups water to a boil. Stir in the rice, return to a boil, reduce heat to low, cover and simmer 25 minutes till rice is cooked but still firm. Fluff with a fork and allow rice to cool completely. In a 2-qt pot, bring 2 cups water to a boil. Stir in the lentils, return to a boil, reduce heat to a low boil and cook only 2 minutes. Drain lentils using a mesh strainer and rinse with cold water to stop them from cooking further. Allow to cool. In a skillet, cook the onion in the 1 Tbsp olive oil 10 minutes until soft.

In a large bowl, whisk the ¼ cup olive oil, orange zest, orange and lemon juices, garlic, salt and pepper. Add the rice and cooked onion, and mix thoroughly. Cover and refrigerate overnight. To serve, add the lentils, apricots, green onions, cilantro and walnuts, then toss and enjoy.

This is a tasty, colorful side dish which complements lamb, fish, chicken and just about anything grilled. Make it a day ahead to allow the flavors to intensify.

Garlic Mashed Cauli

Makes about 3 Cups or 4-5 Servings   Also Veg, V, Grain Free, Egg Free

2	lb cauliflower (1 very large head), 7-8 cups chopped
1	Tbsp unsweetened rice or almond milk
1¾	tsp sea salt
1¼-1½	tsp garlic powder
½	tsp ghee, optional
½	cup white beans such as cannellini or navy beans, rinsed well using a strainer and drained on a paper towel

My version of low-glycemic mashed potatoes. They taste like you're cheating and getting away with something decadent. For extra creamy, use coconut milk.

In a 4-qt pot, cook the cauliflower in 5 cups of water, covered, about 10 minutes, until very soft. Drain well using a colander. Into a blender, put the cauliflower with the milk, salt, garlic powder and ghee, if using. Blend on low speed 15 seconds. Scrape sides of blender, push cauliflower down and blend on low again. Repeat as needed. Once cauliflower is coarsely ground, add beans and blend on low speed just until smooth, but not creamed.

Orange Cranberry Sauce

Makes about 5 Cups   Also Veg, V, Grain Free, Egg Free

6	cups fresh cranberries, washed and sorted
1	cup freshly grated orange zest
½	cup fresh-squeezed orange juice
1¼	cups coconut palm sugar
1	tsp liquid stevia

Tangy and sweet, with an infusion of fresh orange. Why buy an overpriced, processed product full of refined white sugar when you can quickly whip this up in advance?

In a 3-qt saucepan, bring all ingredients, except for sugar, to a boil. Lower heat, stir and cook about 10 minutes until most of the cranberries have popped. Remove from heat and stir in sugar. Enjoy hot, at room temperature, or chill before serving.

Herbed Turkey Dressing

Serves 8-10   Also Veg, V & Egg Free (w/ vegetable broth & egg replacer)

2¼   cups chopped yellow or brown onion
3½   cups sliced celery, about 6 stalks
¼   cup olive oil
2   large eggs
1¼   cups chicken stock or broth
1½   tsp ground coriander
1   Tbsp fresh sage or 1 tsp ground
1   Tbsp fresh thyme or ½ tsp dried
2   Tbsp fresh parsley
½   tsp Herbs de Provence, optional
2½   tsp sea salt
½   tsp black pepper
10   cups cubed GF bread
1   cup chopped pecans, optional

What a joy! Now on Thanksgiving or any other day when they pass the dressing, you no longer need to say "no thanks." On top of that, your family will love this dressing without even knowing it's GF.

In a skillet, sauté the onion and celery in the oil over medium-high heat covered, stirring occasionally, until soft. Preheat oven to 375°. Brush a 2½-qt baking dish with grapeseed oil. In a large bowl, whisk the eggs. Whisk in the chicken stock, herbs, spices, salt and pepper. Add onion and celery, including the oil. Stir in bread and pecans, if using, and mix thoroughly until bread has absorbed the liquid. Turn into baking dish, cover and bake 35 minutes.

Snacks & Treats

Herb & Nut Crackers

Makes about 64 Crackers   Also Veg

- ¼ cup coconut oil (divided 1 Tbsp + 3 Tbsp if using fresh garlic & herbs)
- 1 Tbsp minced fresh sage or ¾ tsp ground
- 1 Tbsp minced fresh thyme or 1 tsp dried
- 1 large clove garlic, pressed or 1⅛ tsp garlic powder
- ⅓ cup almond meal
- 1 cup + 2 Tbsp brown rice flour
- ¼ cup tapioca flour
- 1⅛ tsp sea salt
- 1⅛ tsp xanthan gum
- 2 large eggs
- 2 Tbsp water
- 3 Tbsp dehydrated minced onion
- ⅓ cup finely chopped almonds
- ⅓ cup finely chopped walnuts
- • parchment paper

If using fresh herbs and garlic, in a small skillet, cook sage, thyme and garlic in 1 Tbsp of oil over low heat 2 minutes. Remove from heat and set aside. If using dried herbs and garlic, add them to flour mixture. Preheat oven to 350°. In a large bowl, whisk together almond meal, two flours, herbs (if using dried), salt and xanthan gum. With a large spoon, mix 3 remaining Tbsp oil (if using fresh herbs & garlic) or entire ¼ cup (if using dried) into flour mixture, stirring and pressing with back of spoon till evenly mixed. In a small bowl, whisk eggs, water and onion. Stir egg mixture into flour mixture till texture is consistent. Stir in nuts and herbs, if using fresh, with the oil they cooked in from skillet. Roll the dough between 2 sheets of parchment paper to ¹⁄₁₆" thick. Remove top sheet and place bottom sheet with dough onto a baking sheet. Use a knife or a pizza cutter to cut 1½" squares. Bake 18-20 minutes till golden. Blot any excess oil with a paper towel. Cool on a rack.

If using fresh garlic & herbs, you will cook them in 1 Tbsp of the ¼ cup coconut oil. If using dried garlic & herbs, you will stir in the ¼ cup oil all at once.

What a treat! Yummy, crunchy, delicious crackers that are healthy & replace the junky, processed, hydrolyzed, starchy crackers of the past.

Basil Hummus

Makes 4 Cups   Also Veg, V, Grain Free, Egg Free

- 2 15 oz cans garbanzo beans, rinsed and drained well
- 2 cloves garlic or 2½ tsp garlic powder
- 1½ tsp sea salt
- ½ cup tahini
- ½ cup fresh lemon juice
- ¾ cup water
- 2 Tbsp olive oil
- 1 cup moderately packed fresh basil leaves
- • optional toppings: raw or toasted pine nuts, extra minced basil

Blend all ingredients, except for basil and toppings, on low until mixed. (Begin with ½ cup water.) Add basil and blend on medium until smooth. If it seems too thick, add water 1 Tbsp at a time. Then blend on high (medium if using a high-speed blender) for a creamy smooth texture. Garnish with pine nuts and/or minced basil.

This is killer! Already nutritious hummus just got better with the added flavor & nutrient boost of basil which has anti-bacterial and anti-inflammatory properties and is rich in vitamins A, K & C as well as magnesium, iron, potassium and calcium.

Kale Chips

Makes Approx. 8 Cups   Also Veg, V, **Grain Free**, Egg Free

- 7 cups moderately packed, washed and thoroughly dried kale, stems removed and torn into approximately 2½" x 2½" pieces
- 2 Tbsp olive oil + extra
- ½ tsp sea salt
- 1 tsp garlic powder

One cup of kale, a nutrient dense super food, provides 684% of the RDA of vitamin K, 206% of vitamin A and 134% of vitamin C. Kale is also high in antioxidants, is thought to have cancer-fighting qualities, and does wonders for alkalizing our pH.

Preheat oven to 300°. Line a baking sheet with parchment paper or brush it lightly with olive oil. In a large bowl, toss the torn kale pieces with the oil. Sprinkle with the salt & garlic powder. Rub the pieces lightly between your fingers to make sure that each piece is coated. Spread them out on the baking sheet in a single layer. Bake approximately 10 minutes. Check to see that the chips are crispy but not burnt. When chips are crispy, remove from oven, cool and munch away.

Lightly crispy & fabulous! It's amazing that an incredibly healthy vegetable like kale can be so quickly & easily transformed into a substitute for the much loved, but unhealthy chips made from potato or corn. There is absolutely no guilt in eating these. Consider them a necessary health supplement. :) Change up the flavor with an array of seasonings & herbs. Try cayenne pepper, chili powder, chipotle pepper, lemon pepper or dill. I love them best with just the sea salt & garlic powder.

Cashew Cheese

Makes 2 cups   Also Veg, V, Grain Free, Egg Free

- 2   cups raw unsalted cashews
- 2-4 Tbsp water, depending on desired consistency
- 3   Tbsp fresh lemon juice
- 1   tsp sea salt
- 2   medium cloves garlic, or 1 tsp garlic powder

Okay, this is amazing! For all of us who no longer eat cheese, but have missed it terribly, we can now enjoy what tastes like & seems like a fabulous soft cheese. It takes 5 minutes to prepare, all done in a blender! What's more, unlike other diary substitutes made of undesirable white starches, soy or chemicals, Cashew Cheese is not a compromise in eating healthy because it simply consists of 4 nutritious, real foods.

Soak the cashews in 2 cups of water for at least 2 hours if your blender is powerful, or longer (4-8 hours) for a less powerful blender. This will cause the nuts to blend into a creamier texture. Rinse the nuts using a wire mesh strainer and drain on a paper towel. Into a **high-speed blender,** pour all of the ingredients. Blend on high until the consistency is very smooth and creamy. Use a silicone spatula to scrape down the sides of the blender when necessary. Transfer the mixture to a 3-4 cup container, cover and refrigerate. The Cashew Cheese will firm up in 4-5 hours and will be firmer still after being chilled 8-10 hours.

Red Pepper Almond Dip

Makes 3½ cups   Also Veg, V, Grain Free, Egg Free

½ cup grapeseed oil	3-4 large cloves garlic
1½ cups raw almonds	1½ tsp sea salt
2 cups chopped red bell pepper	¾ tsp onion powder
(1½ large peppers) +	15 oz can garbanzo beans, rinsed
extra for garnish	and drained
1½ Tbsp water	¼ tsp smoked paprika or ¼ tsp
2 Tbsp fresh lemon juice	cayenne pepper, optional

Into a **high-speed blender,** pour only the oil and almonds and blend until smooth. Scrape down the sides of blender as needed. Add the bell pepper, water, lemon juice, garlic, salt and onion powder, and blend until smooth. Last, add the beans and blend. Garnish with a little diced red bell pepper and a sprinkle of paprika or cayenne pepper.

Onion Garlic Almond Dip

Makes 2¾ Cups   Also Veg, V, Grain Free, Egg Free

½ cup + 1 Tbsp grapeseed oil	3 cloves garlic
1½ cups raw almonds	1½ tsp sea salt
¼ cup water	½ cup garbanzo beans, rinsed and drained
¾ cup chopped brown onion	• tsp red chili flakes for garnish
2 Tbsp fresh lemon juice	• optional ½-1 small jalapeno pepper, seeded, for lots of heat

Into a **high-speed blender,** pour only the oil and almonds and blend until smooth. Scrape down the sides of blender as needed. Add the water, onion, lemon juice, garlic and salt, and blend until smooth. Last, add the beans and pepper, if using, and blend. Garnish with a sprinkle of red chili flakes.

Cilantro & Green Onion Almond Dip

Makes 3-4 Cups   Also Veg, V, Grain Free, Egg Free

⅔ cup grapeseed oil	1¼ tsp sea salt
1½ cups raw almonds	1 cup moderately packed fresh cilantro leaves + extra for garnish
½ cup water	¼ cup sliced green onion + extra for garnish
¼ cup fresh lemon juice	½ cup garbanzo beans, rinsed and drained
2 cloves garlic	

Into a **high-speed blender,** pour only the oil and almonds and blend until smooth. Scrape down the sides of blender as needed. Add the water, lemon juice, garlic, salt, cilantro and green onion, and blend until smooth. Last, add the beans and blend. Garnish with a little green onion and cilantro.

Mango Citrus Salsa

3½ cups or 6-8 servings   Also Veg, V, Grain Free, Egg Free, Vinegar Free

1½ cups peeled, chopped mango (about 1½ mangos)
 1 cup chopped red and orange bell peppers
⅓ cup chopped yellow or white onion
 3 Tbsp fresh lime juice
 3 Tbsp cilantro leaves
1/16 tsp sea salt
¾ cup chopped avocado
 • dashes of cayenne pepper, optional

Not only fabulous to top fish & chicken, but a zesty-sweet direction for a green salad with crab! Or, perk up your vegetables with this splash of flavor & color.

In a medium bowl, toss all ingredients together.

Creamy Scallion Sauce

4-5 Servings about 2½ cups   Also Veg, V, Grain Free, Egg Free, Vinegar Free

½ cup grapeseed, sunflower or rice bran oil
2 Tbsp water
⅓ cup fresh lemon juice
1 15 oz can cannellini, navy or Great Northern beans, rinsed and drained on a paper towel

1¾ cups scallions or green onions, chopped in 1" lengths, packed
2 medium cloves garlic or ¾ tsp garlic powder
2 tsp sea salt

Into a blender, put the oil, water, lemon juice and beans. Blend until smooth. Add the onion, garlic and salt, and blend again till creamy. Pour the Scallion Sauce into a 2-qt pot. Heat sauce slowly over low heat, stirring often. Do not boil.

Cilantro Hummus

Makes 4¼ Cups   Also Veg, V, Grain Free, Egg Free

2 15 oz cans garbanzo beans, rinsed and drained well
½ cup tahini
4-6 cloves garlic or 2½ tsp garlic powder
½ cup fresh lemon juice
½-¾ cup water
2 Tbsp olive oil

1¾ tsp sea salt
⅛ tsp cumin
1/16 tsp cayenne pepper
1¼ cups moderately packed fresh cilantro
1 tsp seeded, minced fresh serrano chile, optional

Blend all ingredients, except for cilantro, in a food processor or blender on low until mixed. (Begin with ½ cup water.) Add cilantro and serrano chile, if using, and blend on medium until smooth. If mixture seems too thick, add water 1 Tbsp at a time. Finish by blending on high (**medium** if using a high-speed blender) for a creamy smooth texture.

Flavor galore with the antioxidant benefits provided by cilantro.

Cranberry Quinoa Bars

Makes 22 1½"x3" Bars   Also Veg, **Grain Free**, Egg Free

- 1 cup quinoa flakes, such as Ancient Harvest® brand
- 1 cup lightly toasted buckwheat groats, such as Arrowhead Mills® brand
- 1 cup raw sesame seeds
- 1 cup raw pumpkin seeds
- 1 cup raw sunflower seeds
- ½ cup finely chopped almonds, optional

- 1 cup naturally sweetened cranberries, raisins or other dried fruit
- 1 cup coconut palm sugar
- ¾ cup coconut nectar
- 1 cup + 2 Tbsp sunflower seed butter
- ¼ tsp liquid stevia
- ¼ tsp sea salt

To toast seeds, preheat oven to 350º. Spread seeds out on rimmed baking sheet and bake about 15 minutes. If your seeds are toasted, skip this step. If your buckwheat groats are raw (a light green-tan color), toast by spreading on a rimmed baking sheet and bake only 6 minutes at 350º. This gives them a lighter, softer crunch. Line a 9x13 baking pan with parchment paper, leaving edges long so you can lift it out for easier cutting. Brush parchment paper with grapeseed oil. Measure all ingredients before beginning. In a 3-qt pot, stir the 2 sugars constantly over medium-low heat till sugar dissolves. Bring to a full boil, remove from heat and quickly stir in sunflower seed butter, stevia and salt till well combined. Then add remaining ingredients and mix well. Use a square of wax or parchment paper to press mixture into pan firmly. Refrigerate 2-3 hours before cutting.

Don't think that these energy bars are sensational just because they are chewy, crispy & nut-buttery delicious! Love them more because of their seeds, nuts, buckwheat and quinoa which make them high in protein & fiber, & rich in potassium, iron & magnesium. For even lower sugar, you can eliminate the fruit.

Cinnamon Crunch Oat-Free Granola

Makes 7 Cups   Also Veg, V, **Grain Free**, Egg Free

- ½ cup almond meal
- ¼ cup **whole** buckwheat groats such as Arrowhead Mills® or Pocono® brand
- ⅓ cup quinoa flakes such as Ancient Harvest® brand
- 1 cup chopped walnuts
- 1 cup sliced almonds
- ¼ cup raw sunflower seeds
- 1 Tbsp sesame seeds
- ⅓ cup unsweetened coconut, optional
- ¼ cup + 2 Tbsp water

- ¾ cup coconut palm sugar
- 2 Tbsp ground cinnamon
- ½ tsp ground ginger
- ¼ tsp + ⅛ tsp sea salt

Crispy, crunchy, sweet, wholesome & grain free! This granola is more than a yummy treat. It's packed with nutrition, fiber & protein plus the wonderful flavor & anti-inflammatory benefits of cinnamon & ginger.

Preheat oven to 350º. Brush a rimmed baking sheet generously with grapeseed oil or use parchment paper. In a large bowl, mix the first 8 ingredients. In a 1-qt saucepan, stir the sugar into the water and bring to a boil over medium-low heat, stirring often. Cook 30 seconds more after it boils and remove from heat. Stir in the cinnamon, ginger and salt. Pour over the dry ingredients and mix thoroughly. Spread out evenly and not too thickly on the baking sheet and bake 18 minutes. Cool 15 minutes and then loosen with a spatula before allowing it to finish cooling. It will continue to crisp up as it cools.

Berry Green Smoothie

Makes 24 oz   Also Veg, V, Grain Free, Egg Free

1½	cups moderately packed raw kale or deep green blend such as chard, spinach or beet greens
1¼-1½	Tbsp ground cinnamon
2	dashes sea salt
2	Tbsp chia seeds
¼-⅓	tsp liquid stevia, to taste
2	cups frozen berry combination such as strawberries, blueberries, raspberries
1	cup chilled 100% unsweetened cranberry juice, such as Trader Joe's®
⅔	cup water –or– ⅓ cup water with ⅓ cup plain or vanilla hemp milk
4-5	ice cubes
	Optional: 3-4 Tbsp white beans for protein boost, additional fiber and a creamy flavor
	Optional: ½-1 Tbsp hemp seeds for protein boost and additional fiber

Put all ingredients into a blender made for making smoothies such as a NutriBullet® or into a powerful blender. Blend until smooth. Note: These amounts should fit in a NutriBullet®. Stir in a little more water after blending, if desired.

This Smoothie is actually sweet & berry-flavored. It is a delicious way to enjoy the antioxidant benefits of berries and phytonutrient-rich deep greens, plus the extraordinary boon of fiber-rich chia seeds, and the antioxidant/anti-inflammatory boost of cinnamon.

Chocolate Chip Muffins

Makes 12 Muffins   Also Veg, **Grain Free**

2	large eggs	¾	cup coconut palm sugar
1½	tsp liquid stevia	⅓	cup sunflower seed butter
2	tsp vanilla	2	tsp aluminum-free, GF baking powder
2	Tbsp unsweetened apple sauce	1½	tsp baking soda
2	tsp ghee, melted	¼	tsp + ⅛ tsp sea salt
2	15 oz cans cannellini beans, rinsed well using a wire strainer and drained on a paper towel	½	cup DF dark chocolate chips*
		•	parchment paper

Preheat oven to 350°. Brush a muffin tin with grapeseed oil and lay a 1¼" square of parchment paper in each muffin cup, or use paper liners. If using a high-speed blender, use **medium** speed. For a standard blender, use high speed. Into the blender, put the eggs, stevia, vanilla, apple sauce and ghee and blend 20 seconds. Add the rest of the ingredients and blend 30 seconds. Scrape sides of blender and blend 1½ minutes. Stir in the chocolate chips and fill muffin cups ¾ full. Bake 21 minutes or until tops are firm and a toothpick comes out clean. Cool on a rack 5 minutes, then run a knife around the edges and turn muffins out to finish cooling on the rack.

* See suggested chocolate chips in "Stocking your GF, DF, SF Pantry," p.5

A fun treat! The kids will think they're getting away with something, but they haven't read the ingredients. It'll be our secret!

Cookies & Bars

Espresso Chocolate Macadamia Cookies

Makes 24 Cookies   Also Veg

¾ cup grapeseed oil

1¼ cups coconut palm sugar

2 large eggs

¼ cup decaf coffee crystals

1 tsp vanilla

1⅛ tsp liquid stevia

1⅛ tsp sea salt

1½ tsp aluminum-free, GF baking powder

1 tsp baking soda

⅓ cup cocoa powder

1 tsp xanthan gum

1¼ cups brown rice flour

2½ Tbsp coconut flour

1 cup almond **flour**

½ cup halved or chopped raw macadamia nuts

½ cup DF dark chocolate chips*

These chewy, rich cookies satisfy the love of coffee, chocolate and cookies all in one.

Please note that this recipe calls for almond **flour, not meal** (see p.3)

Preheat oven to 350º. Brush a baking sheet with grapeseed oil. In a very small bowl, crush the coffee crystals into fine powder with the back of a spoon. In a mixing bowl, whisk the oil and sugar. Add the eggs, decaf powder, vanilla, stevia, salt, baking powder, baking soda, cocoa powder and xanthan gum. Whisk until the sugar has dissolved and consistency is smooth. Stir in the three flours with a wooden spoon. Stir in the nuts and chocolate chips. Dough will be soft and sticky. Rest it for 5 minutes to thicken. Make 1¾" mounds on the baking sheet 1½" apart. Bake 8-9 minutes. Don't over-bake. Cool 3 minutes before removing with spatula.

* See suggested chocolates in "Stocking your GF, DF, SF Pantry," p.5

Lemon Coconut Cookies

Makes 24 Cookies   Also Veg, V, Egg Free

- ½ cup grapeseed oil
- ¼ cup water
- 2 tsp fresh lemon juice
- ¼ cup lemon zest
- 1½ cups coconut palm sugar
- ¼ tsp liquid stevia
- ¾ tsp sea salt
- 1½ tsp aluminum-free, GF baking powder
- 1 tsp baking soda
- 1 tsp xanthan gum
- 2 cups almond meal
- 1½ cups brown rice flour
- 1 cup chopped walnuts
- ¾ cup unsweetened, small flake coconut

Chewy, lemony-sweet with sprinkles of coconut, this wonderfully-fresh take on cookies is so good they'll disappear quickly.

Preheat oven to 325°. Brush a baking sheet with grapeseed oil. In a large bowl, whisk together the first 10 ingredients. With a spoon, stir in the remaining ingredients and form 1¾" balls on the baking sheet. Bake 16-18 minutes. Cool on a rack.

Almond Walnut Bars

Makes 32 Bars   Also Veg, V, Egg Free

2¼   cups brown rice flour
¼   cup tapioca flour
1   cup almond meal
2   tsp sea salt
2   tsp xanthan gum
¾   cup coconut oil, softened
½   cup coconut nectar
1   tsp liquid stevia
1   tsp almond extract
2   Tbsp water
¾   cup finely chopped almonds
¾   cup finely chopped walnuts

If you love nuts, this is the cookie for you! Toasty, crunchy almonds & walnuts star in this treat. Nutritionally speaking, almonds are the best nut, packed with vitamins, minerals, protein & fiber, but walnuts are a close second. Recent studies suggest that almonds reduce the risk of colon cancer and walnuts reduce the risk of prostate & breast cancer. Both nuts assist in heart and brain health.

Preheat oven to 350°. Brush a 9x13 baking pan with grapeseed oil. In a large bowl, whisk flours, almond meal, salt and xanthan gum together. Add the coconut oil. Mix well, using a large spoon, taking time to press and stir dough until it becomes consistently moistened. Stir in the coconut nectar, stevia, almond extract and water until well combined. Add the nuts and knead the dough a couple times with your hands. Turn dough into the baking pan and press down firmly until it is even and flat. Bake 18-20 minutes until cookies are golden. Cool on a rack 15 minutes and cut into bars.

"Peanut" Butter Crispy Bars

Makes 20-24   Also Veg, V, Egg Free, Peanut Free

1   cup coconut palm sugar
¾   cup coconut nectar
1¼   cups sunflower seed butter
¼   tsp liquid stevia
¼   tsp sea salt

6   cups 100% crispy brown rice, such as Barbara's®
Chocolate Topping: either
•   12 oz melted DF dark chocolate chips, p.5 -or-
•   Chocolate Candy Topping, p.167

Brush a 9x13 baking dish with grapeseed oil. Before starting, measure all ingredients because you will need to move quickly. Into a 4-qt pot, pour the 2 sugars and stir over medium-high heat constantly till sugar dissolves. Bring to a full boil, remove from heat and quickly stir in the sunflower seed butter, stevia and salt till well combined. Add rice and mix thoroughly. Turn into baking dish and press down evenly using a square of wax paper. Allow to cool. Top with either of the 2 chocolate topping options. Refrigerate 2-3 hours before cutting.

My Mother-In-Law is renown (especially in our family) for her Peanut Butter Crispy Bars. So, I came up with this GF, DF, SF version of her special treat. Always a winner—a big hit with everyone!

143

German Chocolate Black Bean Brownies

Makes 12 Brownies   Also Veg, **Grain Free**

Coconut Pecan Frosting (make this first):

3   large egg yolks, whisked
1½ cups **whole** coconut milk
3   Tbsp ghee, softened
¾   cup + 2 Tbsp coconut palm sugar
1   tsp vanilla

⅛   tsp sea salt
⅛   tsp liquid stevia
1½ cups unsweetened coconut
1½ cups chopped pecans

Preheat oven to 350°. Spread a little more than 1½ cups pecans on a baking sheet and bake 5 minutes until golden. Cool, then chop and measure 1½ cups. In a 2-qt pot, whisk the egg yolks, milk, ghee and sugar. Set the pan on medium heat and stir briskly with the whisk for 12 minutes. The mixture will bubble and thicken. Remove from heat and stir in the vanilla, salt and stevia. With a spoon, stir in the coconut and pecans. Cover and refrigerate 2 hours or until it thickens enough to frost the brownies.

Brownies:

2   large eggs
1   Tbsp water
⅓   cup grapeseed oil
1½ tsp vanilla
¾   tsp liquid stevia
1   15 oz can black beans, rinsed well using
    a wire strainer and drained on a paper towel
1¼ cups coconut palm sugar

2   Tbsp coconut nectar
¾   cup unsweetened cocoa powder
¼   tsp sea salt
1½ tsp aluminum-free, GF baking powder
1   tsp baking soda
¾   tsp xanthan gum
½   cup dark chocolate chips or chunks, optional*

Preheat oven to 350°. Brush an 8x11 pan with grapeseed oil. An immersion blender works well with this recipe.** If using a high-speed blender, use **medium** speed. For a standard blender or food processor, use high speed. Blend the eggs, water, oil, vanilla and stevia 10 seconds, then add the beans and blend 30 seconds. Scrape sides of the blender as needed. Add all remaining ingredients except for the chocolate chips or chunks. Process 1-2 minutes until thoroughly blended. Stir in the chocolate chips or chunks, if using. Pour the batter into the pan and bake 24-26 minutes, or until a toothpick comes out clean. Cool completely on a wire rack and then frost.

* See suggested chocolates in "Stocking your GF, DF, SF Pantry," p.5

** If you have an immersion blender, mix everything in a large bowl instead of in a blender. Use the blending wand for the first 6 ingredients, and then the whisk attachment or a hand mixer for the remainder.

Rich, chewy, coconut & pecan German Chocolate Brownies.
No one would ever know or probably believe you if you told
them that they're made out of black beans!

Raspberry Swirl Black Bean Brownies

Makes 12 Brownies   Also Veg, **Grain Free**

Raspberry Sauce:

- 1   cup fresh or frozen (defrosted) raspberries
- 10 drops liquid stevia
- 1/32 tsp xanthan gum (this is 1/4 of 1/8 tsp and all you need)

Brownies:

- 2   large eggs
- 1/3 cup grapeseed oil
- 1½ tsp vanilla
- 3/4 tsp liquid stevia
- 1   15 oz can black beans, rinsed well using a wire strainer and drained on a paper towel
- 1¼ cups coconut palm sugar

- 2   Tbsp coconut nectar
- 3/4 cup unsweetened cocoa powder
- 1/4 tsp sea salt
- 1½ tsp aluminum-free, GF baking powder
- 1   tsp baking soda
- 3/4 tsp xanthan gum
- 1/2 cup dark chocolate chips or chunks, optional*

Into a blender or smaller device like a NutriBullet®, put the raspberries and stevia, and blend briefly on medium. Add the xanthan gum (a very tiny amount, but all you need). Blend again briefly until smooth and set aside. Preheat oven to 350°. Brush an 8x11 pan with grapeseed oil. An immersion blender works well with this recipe.** If using a high-speed blender, use **medium** speed. For a standard blender or food processor, use high speed. Blend the eggs, oil, vanilla and stevia 10 seconds, then add the beans and blend 30 seconds. Scrape sides of the blender as needed. Add all remaining ingredients except for the chocolate chips or chunks and the raspberry sauce. Process 1-2 minutes until thoroughly blended. Stir in the chocolate chips or chunks, if using. Spread the batter into the pan. A silicone spatula is very helpful to get all the batter out of the blender. Drop spoonfuls of the raspberry sauce evenly over the top. With a knife, swirl back and forth across the pan from one end to the other, one time, to work the sauce down into the batter. Don't overwork it. Sprinkle with extra chocolate chips if desired and bake 30 minutes or until a toothpick comes out clean. Cool completely on a wire rack.

*See suggested chocolates in "Stocking your GF, DF, SF Pantry," p.5

** If you have an immersion blender, mix everything in a large bowl instead of a blender. Use the blending wand for the first 6 ingredients, and then the whisk attachment or hand mixer for the remainder.

> Some days, a chewy, rich, dark chocolate brownie with ribbons of tart, sweet raspberries is the best indulgence there could be. Especially Delightful, no one would ever guess that these brownies are grain free and made of black beans.

Holiday Sugar Cookies

Makes 12-16 Cookies   Veg, V, Egg Free, **Dye Free**

- ⅔   cup coconut palm sugar
- ½   cup coconut oil
- 2   Tbsp unsweetened apple sauce
- 2   tsp vanilla
- ¼   tsp liquid stevia
- 1   cup brown rice flour
- ¼   cup arrowroot flour
- ½   cup tapioca flour
- ½   tsp sea salt
- ¾   tsp baking soda
- ½   tsp xanthan gum
- •   parchment paper

Into a blender, put the sugar and blend until it becomes powdery. Line a baking sheet with parchment paper. In a medium-size mixing bowl, with an electric mixer, cream the sugar and coconut oil. Beat in the apple sauce, vanilla and stevia. Add the remaining cookie ingredients and beat. Use your hands or large spoon to press and knead the dough to form a soft lump. Turn lump of dough onto a sheet of parchment paper. Lay a 2nd sheet of parchment paper over the dough. Preheat oven to 350°. Roll the dough between the 2 sheets of parchment paper to ¼" thick. (If dough is rolled thinner, it is difficult to work with.) Use a cookie cutter to make cookie shapes. Refrigerate dough 8 minutes if necessary to make easier to work with. Use a spatula to carefully lift each cookie onto the baking sheet lined with parchment paper. Bake 10 minutes, remove from oven and allow to cool at least 8 minutes before removing. Decorate cookies with Dye-Free Holiday Icing.

Dye-Free Holiday Icing

Frosts 12-16 Cookies

- ¼   cup + 2 Tbsp light coconut milk
- ¼   tsp + ⅛ tsp agar **powder**
- ¼   cup + ½ Tbsp raw honey
- ¼   tsp liquid stevia
- 1½   tsp coconut oil
-   less than ⅛ tsp sea salt
- •   dye-free coloring of your choice
- ¾   cup potato starch
- 1½   Tbsp tapioca starch

Dye-Free Colors:

Pink: 1-2 tsp 100% unsweetened cranberry juice, such as Trader Joe's® brand
Red: 1-2 tsp water from cooking red beets*
Yellow: 1-2 tsp water from cooking golden beets*
Purple: 1-2 tsp water from cooking red cabbage*
Blue: Purple + pinch of baking soda*
Orange: combine red & yellow
Green: combine yellow & blue

Have all ingredients measured before you begin. In a 1-qt pot, whisk the agar into the milk. Set onto low heat and allow it to come to a boil while stirring with whisk 5 minutes. Remove from heat and whisk in the honey, stevia, coconut oil, salt and your choice of dye-free color. With a spoon, stir in the potato starch and tapioca flour. Ice cookies immediately before icing sets.

*In small saucepan, bring ¾ cup water and 2 quartered red beets or 2 quartered golden beets or ½ head red cabbage to a boil. Reduce heat and simmer covered 1 hour, checking often to ensure that the water doesn't evaporate completely. You will end up with 1-2 tablespoons deep red or yellow or purple-colored water. If more than 2 Tbsp remains, remove the lid and continue to cook on low. Remove from heat when there is only about 2 Tbsp of water remaining. Remove the beets/cabbage. To make the purple cabbage water blue, add a pinch of baking soda **after** it has cooled.

Lightly crunchy, sweet and fun, these cookies delight the child in us all. Free of not only gluten, dairy and refined-sugar, but also egg, soy and dye, they're perfect for celebrating every season! Dye-free food colors can also be purchased at health food markets or online.

Thumbprint Cookies

Makes 18 Cookies   Also Veg, V & Egg Free (w/ egg replacer), Peanut Free

½ cup grapeseed oil	1 tsp baking soda
½ cup sunflower seed butter	½ cup almond meal
1 cup coconut palm sugar	½ cup brown rice flour
1 tsp vanilla	¼ cup + 2 Tbsp coconut flour
1 large egg, whisked	18 DF dark chocolate kisses
¾ tsp sea salt	

Preheat oven to 350°. Brush a baking sheet with grapeseed oil. In a bowl, whisk oil, sunflower seed butter, sugar and vanilla until sugar has dissolved. Stir in remaining ingredients. Roll into 1½" balls and place on baking sheet, then press a chocolate kiss into center. Bake 7 minutes for chewy cookies or 9 minutes for crunchy ones.

Peanuts are high on the list of inflammatory foods. For those with inflammation issues or peanut allergies, it's heaven to be able to enjoy these chewy, crunchy peanutty cookies. You'd never know there's not a trace of peanut in them.

Biscotti

Makes 24 Cookies   Also Veg

¼ cup coconut oil	½ cup arrowroot flour
2 tsp ghee	¼ cup unsweetened cocoa powder
1¼ cups coconut palm sugar	1 tsp aluminum-free, GF baking powder
¼ tsp liquid stevia	¼ tsp sea salt
2 eggs	1¼ tsp xanthan gum
1¼ tsp almond extract	1 cup sliced almonds
1¾ cups brown rice flour	• optional toppings below

Preheat oven to 350º. Brush 2 baking sheets with grapeseed oil. In a large bowl with a mixer, beat oil, ghee, sugar and stevia. Add eggs and almond extract and beat until smooth. In another bowl, whisk together flours, cocoa, baking powder, salt and xanthan gum. Add dry ingredients to wet ingredients and mix well. Stir in the almonds.

Divide dough into two halves. Dampen hands with water to work with dough because it is sticky. Shape each half into 2"x11" logs. Place both logs on a baking sheet and bake on middle rack 30 minutes. Cool 15 minutes. Cut logs into ½" width-wise slices and place slices cut side down on two baking sheets. Reposition oven racks to the top and middle positions. Put one baking sheet on each rack and bake 9-10 minutes. Remove from oven, turn each piece over, return to oven on the opposite rack and bake another 9-10 minutes. Remove from oven and cool.

Optional toppings: Melt 1 cup DF dark chocolate chips with 1 Tbsp coconut oil, stir till smooth. Dip top of each cookie. Refrigerate 10 minutes. Meanwhile, mix ¼ cup melted vanilla chips with 1 tsp coconut oil, stir until smooth. Drizzle over chocolate. Or Chocolate Candy Topping, p.167. Dip top of each cookie. Refrigerate 10 minutes, then use Holiday Cookie Icing without the dye-free color, p.149. Drizzle over chocolate.

Festive Biscotti for Christmas! My sis-in-law & niece are known for their fabulous Biscotti. One year they asked me to convert their traditional recipe into a GF, DF, refined SF version which I was Delighted to do. We came up with beautiful, authentic Biscotti, GF, DF & SF.

Pies, Cakes & Desserts

Raspberry "Cheesecake" 🗋

Makes One 9" (or 10") Pie   Also Veg, V, Grain Free (w/o crust), Egg Free

- 4 cups raw, unsalted cashews
- ¼ cup coconut oil, melted
- ½ cup raw honey
- ¾ tsp liquid stevia
- 1½ tsp vanilla
- ½ cup + 1 tsp fresh lemon juice
- ¼ tsp + ⅛ tsp sea salt
- 1 cup fresh raspberries or 2 cups frozen, thawed + raspberries to garnish
- 1 Tbsp additional raw honey
- ¾ tsp additional liquid stevia
- 1 9" **baked** pie crust, 3 choices, p.156-157 (Sweet Nut Crust in photo)

It's heavenly! Your friends & family will never guess, & might not believe even if you tell them that this Raspberry "Cheesecake" is not only free of dairy, but refined sugar & gluten too. Even better, the ingredients are natural, wholesome & high in protein.

Measure 4 cups of cashews and soak them in 3½ cups water for at least 2 hours if your blender is powerful, or longer (4-8 hours) for a less powerful blender. This will cause the nuts to soften and blend into a creamier texture. The cashews will expand to more than 4 cups. Use them all. Rinse the nuts using a wire mesh strainer and drain well on a paper towel.

Put the nuts with all of the ingredients except for the last 3 (the raspberries, additional 1 Tbsp honey and additional ¾ tsp liquid stevia) into a **high-speed blender** and blend on high 1-2 minutes scraping sides of blender as needed until the texture is very soft and creamy. Pour ½ of the mixture into the baked pie crust. There should be about 2¼ cups to pour into the crust with about 2¼ cups left in the blender. Cover and refrigerate the crust with first layer. Add only 1 cup raspberries (2 cups frozen raspberries should equal 1 cup once thawed), and the additional 1 Tbsp honey and the additional ¾ tsp stevia. Blend just until the texture is smooth. Pour the raspberry mixture into the crust over the first layer. Cover and chill at least 8 hours, or best over night. Garnish with additional raspberries, or Naturally Sweetened Berry Syrup, p.67 & chocolate shavings as in photo, if desired.

Whipped Topping

Makes 2 Cups   Also Veg, V, Grain Free, Egg Free

- 1 13½ or 14 oz can **whole** coconut milk
- 15 drops liquid stevia*
- • less than ¹⁄₁₆ tsp sea salt
- ½ tsp xanthan gum
- • optional 2 tsp coconut nectar (which if used will tint whipped topping a shade darker)

What a treat! This seems to defy the DF, SF rule, yet is surprisingly *Delightfully Free*. The perfect touch to complement Pumpkin Pie, Chocolate Decadence Pie, crumble recipes, the Mousse or anything enhanced by whipped cream.

Into a blender, pour the milk, only 15 drops of stevia*, salt, xanthan gum and the coconut nectar if using. Use the lowest speed on blender, such as "stir," 10 seconds. Scrape the sides of blender and blend on a higher speed 40 seconds. Pour into a 2 cup container with a lid and chill for 2 hours. It will continue to thicken as it chills.

*Be careful adding the stevia. It is very sweet and can overpower this delicate topping. Add only 4-5 drops at a time and taste.

Allow 2 hours to chill, then enjoy!

"Cheesecake" 🥤

Makes One 9" pie **Also Veg, V, Grain Free (w/o crust), Egg Free**

4	cups raw, unsalted cashews	½	cup + 1 Tbsp fresh lemon juice
¼	cup coconut oil, melted	¼	tsp + ⅛ tsp sea salt
7	Tbsp raw honey (¼ cup + 2 Tbsp)	1	9" **baked** pie crust, 3 choices, p.156-157
¾	tsp liquid stevia		(Chocolate Nut Crust shown in photo)
1½	tsp vanilla	•	toppings, suggested below

Measure 4 cups of cashews and soak them in 3½ cups water for at least 2 hours if your blender is powerful, or longer (4-8 hours) for a less powerful blender. This will cause the nuts to soften and blend into a creamier texture. Rinse the nuts using a wire mesh strainer and drain well on a paper towel. The cashews will expand to more than 4 cups. Use them all.

Put the nuts with all of the remaining ingredients into a **high-speed blender** and blend on high 1-2 minutes until the texture is very soft and creamy. Scrape sides of blender as needed. Pour into the baked Basic Pie Crust, p.157, Sweet Nut Crust, p.156, or Chocolate Nut Crust, p.156, and chill in the refrigerator for at least 8 hours or best overnight. Slice and enjoy, or top with your choice of fruit, Naturally Sweetened Berry Syrup, p.67, Crumble Topping, p.83 .

Chocolate "Cheesecake" 🥤

Makes One 9" Pie **Also Veg, V, Grain Free (w/o crust), Egg Free**

4	cups raw, unsalted cashews	⅓	cup lemon juice
¼	cup coconut oil, melted	¾	cup coconut palm sugar
¾	tsp liquid stevia	4	oz unsweetened baking chocolate (cocoa mass)
1	Tbsp vanilla	1	9" **baked** pie crust, 3 choices, p.156-157
¼	tsp + ⅛ tsp sea salt		(Sweet Nut Crust shown in photo)

Measure 4 cups of cashews and soak them in 3½ cups water for at least 2 hours if your blender is powerful, or longer (4-8 hours) for a less powerful blender. This will cause the nuts to soften and blend into a creamier texture. Rinse the nuts using a wire mesh strainer and drain well on a paper towel. The cashews will expand to more than 4 cups. Use them all.

Into a **high-speed blender**, pour the oil, stevia, vanilla, salt, lemon juice and sugar. Blend briefly to melt the coconut sugar. Add the drained cashews and blend 1-2 minutes until smooth and creamy, scraping down sides of blender as needed. In a double boiler or a 2-qt saucepan sitting atop a smaller pan of simmering water, melt the chocolate. Remove from heat. Turn blender onto lowest speed. Remove lid and pour the melted chocolate into blender as it blends on low. Use a silicone spatula to scrape in all the chocolate from the pan. Once thoroughly blended, pour into the baked Basic Pie Crust, p.157, Sweet Nut Crust, p.156, or Chocolate Nut Crust, p.156, and chill in the refrigerator for at least 8 hours or best overnight. Slice and enjoy, or top with berries, Naturally Sweetened Berry Syrup, p.67 (as in photo) or Whipped Topping, p.153.

Heavenly, rich & fabulous! It's hard to believe that these "Cheesecakes" are not on our "off limits" list like traditional cheesecakes which are dense with unhealthy fats, too much refined sugar & excessive amounts of dairy & gluten. How sweet it is to eat *Delightfully Free!* 155

SWEET NUT CRUST

Makes One 9" Crust   Also Veg, V, Egg Free

- 1   cup + 2 Tbsp brown rice flour
- 2   Tbsp tapioca flour
- ½   cup almond meal
- 1   tsp sea salt
- 1¼ tsp xanthan gum
- ¼   cup + 2 Tbsp coconut oil, softened
- ¼   cup coconut nectar
- ½   tsp liquid stevia
- 1   Tbsp water
- ⅓   cup finely chopped almonds
- ⅓   cup finely chopped walnuts

Sweet Nut Crust adds great texture, crunch & nutrition to anything you put in a pie crust.

Preheat oven to 350°. Brush a 9" pie dish with grapeseed oil. In a medium bowl, whisk flours, almond meal, salt and xanthan gum together. Add the coconut oil. Mix well, using a large spoon, taking time to press and stir dough until it becomes consistently moistened. Add the coconut nectar, stevia and water. Stir until well combined. Stir in the nuts and knead the dough a couple times with your hands. Turn dough into the prepared pie dish. If pre-baking the crust before filling it, bake 16-18 minutes until the edges turn golden. Cool completely on a rack.

CHOCOLATE NUT CRUST

Makes One 9" Crust   Also Veg, V, Egg Free

- ¾   cup + 2 Tbsp brown rice flour
- 2   Tbsp tapioca flour
- 1   tsp sea salt
- 1   cup unsweetened cocoa powder
- 1½ tsp xanthan gum
- ¼   cup + 2 Tbsp coconut oil, softened
- ¼   cup coconut nectar
- ¾   tsp liquid stevia
- 1½ Tbsp water
- ⅔   cup finely chopped almonds, walnuts or other nut

Yum! This Chocolate Pie Crust is like eating a big, crunchy chocolate cookie plus whatever delicious filling you have selected. Try it with the "Cheesecake", p.155, or with Blueberry Banana "Cream" Pie from p.149 of the original *Delightfully Free* Cookbook or the Rhubarb or Peach Filling from p.155 of the original *Delightfully Free* Cookbook.

Preheat oven to 350°. Brush a 9" pie dish or 4-6 ramekins with grapeseed oil. In a medium bowl, whisk the flours, salt, cocoa powder and xanthan gum together. Add the coconut oil. Mix well, using a large spoon, taking time to press and stir the dough until it becomes consistently moistened. Add the coconut nectar, stevia and water. Stir until well combined. Stir in the nuts and knead the dough a couple times with your hands. Turn dough into the pie dish and press evenly up the sides and onto the lip. If pre-baking the crust before filling it, bake 12 minutes. Cool completely on a rack, or fill and bake as directed.

Basic Pie Crust

Makes One 9" Crust or One 10" Crust   Also Veg, V, Egg Free

9 Inch Crust:
- 1½ cups brown rice flour
- ¼ cup tapioca flour
- 1¹⁄₁₆ tsp sea salt
- ½ tsp + ⅛ tsp cinnamon
- 1 tsp xanthan gum
- ⅓ cup + 1 Tbsp coconut oil, softened
- 3 Tbsp coconut nectar
- 6 drops liquid stevia
- 2 tsp water

10 Inch Crust:
- 2 cups brown rice flour
- ⅓ cup tapioca flour
- 1⅓ tsp sea salt
- 1 tsp cinnamon
- 1⅓ tsp xanthan gum
- ½ cup + 1½ tsp coconut oil, softened
- ¼ cup coconut nectar
- 8 drops liquid stevia
- 2½ tsp water

No need to roll these crusts. They're quick and easy to make and taste like the wonderful pie crusts we fondly remember and miss like crazy!

Preheat oven to 350°. Brush or spray a 9" or 10" pie dish with grapeseed oil. In a medium bowl, whisk flours, salt, cinnamon and xanthan gum together. Add the coconut oil. Mix well, using a large spoon, taking time to press and stir dough until it becomes consistently moistened. Add the coconut nectar, stevia and water. Stir until well combined. Turn dough into the prepared pie dish and, using your hands or the back of a spoon, bring it all the way up the sides and onto the lip of the dish. If pre-baking the crust before filling it, bake crust 14-16 minutes, until light golden. Cool completely on a rack.

Savory Nut Crust

Makes One 9" Crust   Also Veg

- 1⅓ cups brown rice flour
- ¼ cup almond meal
- 3 Tbsp tapioca flour
- 1⅛ tsp sea salt
- 1⅛ tsp xanthan gum
- 1 Tbsp + 3 Tbsp coconut oil
- 1 Tbsp minced fresh sage or ½ tsp ground

- 1 Tbsp minced fresh thyme or 1 tsp dried
- 1 lg clove garlic, pressed, or 1⅛ tsp garlic powder
- 2 large eggs
- 2 Tbsp water
- 3 Tbsp dehydrated minced onion
- ⅓ cup finely chopped almonds
- ⅓ cup finely chopped walnuts

In a small skillet, cook the fresh sage, thyme and garlic in 1 Tbsp of the oil over very low heat for 2 minutes. Remove from heat and set aside. (If using dried herbs and garlic, add them to the flour mixture.) Preheat oven to 350°. Brush a 9" pie dish with grapeseed oil. In a large bowl, whisk together the 2 flours and almond meal, herbs, if using dried, salt and xanthan gum. With a large spoon, mix the 3 Tbsp oil into the flour mixture, stirring and pressing with the back of the spoon till evenly mixed. (Or if using dried herbs, mix in ¼ cup oil.) In a small bowl, whisk the eggs. Whisk in the water and dehydrated minced onion. Stir the egg mixture and herbs from the skillet with all of the oil they cooked in into the flour mixture till texture is consistent. Stir in nuts. Press into pie dish. If pre-baking before filling, bake 25 minutes till edges are golden, or fill and bake as directed.

The kitchen smells so good! Lovely herbs & onion waft throughout the house as you bake anything from quiches, p.73, 77 to Chicken Pot Pie, p.11 in this delicious crust.

German Chocolate Cake

Makes One 9" Layer Cake   Also Veg, **Grain Free**

Coconut Pecan Frosting (make this first):
Frosts and Fills a 2 Layer Cake

6	large egg yolks, whisked
3	cups **whole** coconut milk
¼	cup + 2 Tbsp ghee, softened
1¾	cups coconut palm sugar

2	tsp vanilla
¼	tsp sea salt
⅛	tsp + 7 drops liquid stevia
3	cups unsweetened coconut
3	cups chopped pecans

Preheat oven to 350°. Spread 3¼ cups pecans on a baking sheet and bake 5 minutes until golden. Cool, then chop and measure 3 cups. In a 3-qt pot, whisk the egg yolks, milk, ghee and sugar. Set the pan on medium heat and stir briskly with the whisk for 12 minutes. The mixture will bubble and thicken. Remove from heat and stir in the vanilla, salt and stevia. With a spoon, stir in the coconut and pecans. Cover and refrigerate 2 hours or until it thickens enough to frost the cake or cupcakes.

Makes One 9" Layer

3	large eggs
1	15 oz can black beans, rinsed and drained well on a paper towel
3	Tbsp grapeseed oil
½	cup unsweetened cocoa powder
1½	tsp vanilla
⅛	tsp sea salt

1½	tsp aluminum-free, GF baking powder
1	tsp baking soda
1	cup coconut palm sugar
¾	tsp liquid stevia
1	Tbsp coconut flour
1	Tbsp tapioca flour

Preheat oven to 350°. Brush a 9" cake pan with grapeseed oil, line the bottom of the pan with parchment paper and lightly oil it too. If using a high-speed blender, use **medium** speed. For a standard blender, use high speed. Blend the eggs 10 seconds. Add the beans and blend 1 minute. Add the remaining ingredients and blend on low speed 10 seconds and then on medium or high speed for 1 minute (according to the above directions for your blender type), scraping the sides of blender as needed. Pour batter into the prepared cake pan using a silicone spatula. Bake 22 minutes, or until a toothpick inserted in the center comes out clean and the center of the cake is firm and slightly springy. Cool on a rack 15 minutes. Run a knife around the edge and turn the cake out to cool completely on the rack before frosting.

Chocolate Ganache

Makes ⅔ Cup   Also Veg, V, Grain Free, Egg Free

4	oz unsweetened baking chocolate (cocoa mass)
1	Tbsp + 2 tsp coconut oil
¼	cup coconut nectar

⅛	tsp liquid stevia
2	dashes sea salt

It is best to have all ingredients measured out before beginning. In a double boiler or a 2-qt pan over simmering water, melt the chocolate. Remove from heat and stir in the remaining ingredients till well blended. Spoon the ganache into the circular area on top of the cake to fill it in. Swirl the ganache with the knife as you finish. It will set as it dries.

"Peanut Butter" Chocolate Chip Cake

Makes One 9" Layer   Also Veg, **Grain Free**, Peanut Free

3	large eggs
1	15 oz can cannellini beans, rinsed and drained well on a paper towel
¼	cup sunflower seed butter
2	tsp sesame oil
1½	tsp vanilla
1	tsp liquid stevia
1	cup + 2 Tbsp coconut palm sugar
2	tsp aluminum-free, GF baking powder
1	tsp baking soda
½	tsp sea salt

2	Tbsp tapioca flour
3	Tbsp DF dark chocolate mini chips,* such as Enjoy Life®
⅔	cup finely chopped toasted almonds, optional

Two of my favorite flavors in one delicious cake! This cake has several secrets...one is that though both the cake & the frosting taste like peanut butter, there is none in the recipe. And, like all of the sweet recipes in this book only natural, unrefined, low glycemic sweeteners are used. The biggest surprise is that the cake is actually grain free & the main ingredient is white beans, aka fiber, protein, nutrition!

Preheat oven to 350º. Brush a 9" cake pan with grapeseed oil. Line the bottom of the pan with parchment paper and lightly oil it too. If using a high-speed blender, use **medium** speed. For a standard blender, use high speed. Blend the eggs 10 seconds. Add the beans and blend 1 minute. Add the remaining ingredients except for the chocolate chips and blend briefly. Use a silicone spatula to scrape down sides and blend again for 1 minute. Pour batter into the prepared cake pan, using the silicone spatula. Stir the chocolate chips into the pan. Bake 23 minutes or until a toothpick inserted in the center comes out clean and the center of the cake is firm and slightly springy. Cool on a rack 15 minutes. Run a knife around the edge to loosen before turning the cake out. Allow cake to cool completely on the rack before frosting.

For cupcakes, use paper liners and fill each to almost full, about ¼" from the top. Bake 19-20 minutes. This recipe will make 9 cupcakes.

* See suggested chocolates in "Stocking your GF, DF, SF Pantry," p.5

"Peanut Butter" Frosting

Frosts and Fills a 2 Layer Cake   Also Veg, V, Grain Free, Egg Free, Peanut Free

2½	cups raw unsalted cashews
½	cup coconut oil, melted
½	tsp sesame oil
⅓	cup coconut nectar

1	tsp liquid stevia
¼	tsp + ¹⁄₁₆ tsp sea salt
2	tsp vanilla
2	Tbsp sunflower seed butter

Make a day ahead.

Soak the cashews in 3 cups water for at least 2 hours if your blender is powerful, or longer (4-8 hours) for a less powerful blender. This will cause the nuts to soften and blend into a creamier texture. Rinse the nuts using a wire mesh strainer and drain well on a paper towel. Into a **high-speed blender,** put the nuts and all remaining ingredients. Blend on high until smooth and creamy, scraping the sides of blender as necessary. Transfer to a bowl with a lid and refrigerate 8 hours or best overnight. After frosting has chilled, use a hand mixer to beat the frosting 1-2 minutes. It will become light and fluffy like butter cream frosting. When frosting the cake, if frosting becomes too soft, cover and either put it in the freezer for 15-20 minutes or the refrigerator for an hour. The frosted cake can be left out for a couple of hours but ideally should be refrigerated for longer periods because the frosting will become soft. Times will vary according to the day's temperature.

Spice Cake

Makes One 9" Layer   Also Veg

3	large eggs	2	Tbsp brown rice flour
1	15 oz can cannellini beans, rinsed well using a wire strainer and drained on a paper towel	½	tsp baking soda
¼	cup grapeseed oil	1	Tbsp + 1 tsp aluminum-free, GF baking powder
1½	tsp vanilla	⅛	tsp sea salt
¾	tsp liquid stevia	1¾	tsp ground cinnamon
1	cup + 2 Tbsp coconut palm sugar	1	tsp ground ginger
2	Tbsp tapioca flour	¼	tsp ground cloves
		⅛	tsp ground nutmeg

Preheat oven to 350º. Brush a 9" cake pan with grapeseed oil. Line the bottom of the pan with parchment paper and lightly oil it too. If using a high-speed blender, use **medium** speed. For a standard blender, use high speed. Blend the eggs 10 seconds. Add the beans and blend 1 minute. Add the remaining ingredients and blend briefly. Scrape down sides and blend again for 1 minute. Pour into pan and bake 28-30 minutes or until a toothpick comes out clean & the center of the cake is firm and slightly springy. Cool on a rack 15 minutes. Run a knife around the edge to loosen before turning the cake out. Cool completely on the rack before frosting with "Cream Cheese" Frosting.

For cupcakes, use paper liners and fill to ¼ inch from the top. Bake 19-20 minutes, testing for doneness as directed above. This recipe will make 9 cupcakes.

An old-fashion favorite with a surprising new twist. Yes, this cake is light & moist with the sweet flavor of cinnamon & cloves. But, instead of the traditional white, bleached, processed flour (a non-food that converts to sugar & causes a plethora of other problems), this cake is grain free but for 2 Tbsp of brown rice flour and the main ingredient is white beans! The beans trump flour with the healthy bonuses of being loaded with antioxidants, detoxifying enzymes, fiber & protein.

"Cream Cheese" Frosting

2½	cups raw, unsalted cashews	2¼	tsp liquid stevia
½	cup coconut oil, melted	½	tsp sea salt
3	Tbsp ghee, softened	1	Tbsp white vinegar
½	cup raw honey	2½	Tbsp fresh lemon juice

Make a day ahead.

Soak the cashews in 3 cups water for at least 2 hours if your blender is powerful, or longer (4-8 hours) for a less powerful blender. This will cause the nuts to soften and blend into a creamier texture. Rinse the nuts using a wire mesh strainer and drain well on a paper towel. Into a **high-speed blender,** put the nuts and all remaining ingredients. Blend on high until smooth and creamy, scraping down sides of blender as necessary. Transfer to a bowl, cover and refrigerate 8 hours or best overnight. After frosting has chilled, use an electric mixer to beat the frosting 1-2 minutes. It will become light and fluffy like butter cream frosting. When frosting the cake, if frosting becomes too soft, cover and either put it in the freezer for 15-20 minutes or the refrigerator for an hour. Afterward, the frosting can be beaten again with the electric mixer. The frosted cake can be left out for a couple hours but ideally should be refrigerated for longer periods because the frosting will become soft. Times will vary according to the day's temperature.

Apple Pumpkin Crumble

Serves 8-10   Also Veg, **Grain Free**, Egg Free

Crust & Topping:

⅓   cup + 2 Tbsp grapeseed oil
⅓   cup + 2 Tbsp coconut nectar
1¼ tsp liquid stevia
2½ Tbsp lemon zest
1¼ tsp sea salt
2   Tbsp ground cinnamon
1½ tsp ground ginger
1   Tbsp water
1   cup quinoa flakes such as Ancient Harvest® brand
1   cup almond meal

1   cup toasted* whole buckwheat groats such as Bob's Red Mill® or Pocono® brand
1½ cups chopped toasted almonds
1½ cups chopped toasted walnuts

Filling:

2   cups pureed pumpkin or sweet potato
⅛   tsp sea salt
¾   tsp liquid stevia
½   cup coconut palm sugar
3   cups peeled, finely chopped medium-sweet apple

Apples, cinnamon & pumpkin with a delicious hint of lemon & toasted nuts. While everyone else is enjoying dessert, you can also enjoy knowing that there is a long list of wholesome ingredients that went into it.

Preheat oven to 350°. Brush an 8x11 baking dish with grapeseed oil. In a medium bowl, whisk the first four **filling** ingredients. Stir in the apple. In a large bowl, whisk the first 8 **crust/topping** ingredients. Stir in the quinoa, almond meal, buckwheat & nuts. Press ½ the mixture into the baking dish. Spread the filling over the crust. Spoon remaining topping over filling and press down gently. Cover with a baking sheet and bake 25 minutes. Cool 15 minutes and serve with Cashew Whipped "Cream", p.173 or Whipped Topping, p.153.

*If your buckwheat groats are not toasted (still a greenish-tan color), toast them by spreading on a rimmed baking sheet and bake only 6 minutes at 350°.

Lemon Orange Teacake

Makes One 8x8 Cake   Also Veg, **Grain Free** (w/o brown rice flour*)

4   large eggs
2⅓ cups cannellini beans, rinsed and drained on a paper towel
¼   cup grapeseed oil
3   Tbsp tapioca flour
3   Tbsp arrowroot flour
3   Tbsp brown rice flour
1½ Tbsp baking powder
1½ tsp baking soda

¼   tsp sea salt
1   cup coconut palm sugar
1½ tsp liquid stevia
2   Tbsp fresh lemon juice
1   tsp organic orange extract
3   Tbsp orange zest
•   parchment paper
•   Orange Icing, p.59
2   Tbsp finely grated orange peel, optional

Lovely, lemon-orange sunshine in a moist, light cake that makes any occasion special (never mind that the ingredients are nutritious foods)!

Preheat oven to 350°. Brush an 8x8 baking pan with grapeseed oil, line bottom with parchment paper and brush it with a little oil. If using a high-speed blender, use **medium** speed. For a standard blender, use high speed. Blend eggs 10 seconds. Add beans and blend 1 minute. Add remaining ingredients and blend 1 minute, scraping sides of blender as needed. Pour into pan and bake 30 minutes or until the top is firm and slightly springy and a toothpick comes out clean. Cool on a rack 15 minutes, run a knife around the edges and turn cake out or leave in pan. Cool completely. Ice with Orange Icing and sprinkle with grated orange peel if desired.

*Eliminating the brown rice flour makes the cake moister (a little less cakey). Increase bake time by 3-5 minutes & test for doneness as directed.

Nougat Crunchies

Makes 24   Also Veg, V, Grain Free (w/o cereal*), Peanut Free

½   cup coconut palm sugar
¼   cup + 2 Tbsp coconut nectar
½   cup + 2 Tbsp sunflower seed butter
⅛   tsp sea salt
16   drops liquid stevia
¾   cup whole raw or toasted almonds
¾   cup roasted green peas
½   cup roasted chick peas
½   cup crispy brown rice — or — GF O's — or — Crunchy Flax Cereal
•   wax or parchment paper

Chocolate Topping, optional:
•   ¾ cup melted DF dark chocolate chips, see Chocolates, p.5
•   Chocolate Candy Topping on this page

Chocolate Candy Topping
3   oz unsweetened baking chocolate (cocoa mass)
1   tsp coconut oil
3   Tbsp coconut nectar
10   drops liquid stevia
2   dashes sea salt

Line a baking sheet with wax paper or parchment paper. Measure all ingredients before you begin because you will need to move quickly. Into a 3-qt pot, pour the 2 sugars and stir over medium-high heat until sugar dissolves. Allow mixture to come to a boil, remove from heat and stir in the sunflower seed butter, salt and stevia till well combined. Quickly stir in the remaining ingredients and form 1¾" mounds on the wax paper. Allow to cool. If using chocolate, choose from either of the 2 chocolate toppings suggested above.

Chocolate Candy Topping:

(The Nougat Crunchies or other candy must be made and cooled before beginning.) In a double boiler or a 1-qt pan over a smaller pan of simmering water, melt the chocolate. Remove from heat. Stir in the remaining ingredients and pour over the candy or anything else enhanced by chocolate.

Chewy nougat with chocolate & crunch, made *Delightfully Free* & from healthy, nutritious food! Sunflower seed butter: high in protein & fiber, low in saturated fat, with no cholesterol. Almonds: high in protein & fiber. Green Peas: nutrient dense, high in anti-oxidants. Chick peas: high in protein, fiber & anti-oxidants, anti-inflammatory. A small amount of a wholesome whole grain cereal (*which you can replace with additional nuts or seeds to make the recipe grain free.)

Chocolate Ice Cream 🍶

Makes 2¾ Cups   Also Veg, V, Grain Free, Egg Free

1	cup **whole** coconut milk
3	Tbsp unsweetened cocoa powder
¼	cup coconut nectar or raw honey
½	tsp liquid stevia
1½	tsp vanilla
¼	tsp + ⅛ tsp sea salt
2½	cups ice cubes (not crushed ice)

Delicious using only pure, healthy ingredients. (Have you checked the ingredient label of store bought ice cream?!) For variety, top with "Naturally Sweetened Berry Syrup" on page 67. Or, stir in sunflower seed or almond butter for Chocolate "Peanut Butter" Ice Cream. Stir in decaf coffee crystals & chopped almonds for Almond Mocha Ice Cream.

Into a **high-speed blender,** put milk and cocoa powder. Blend until cocoa powder has dissolved. Add remaining ingredients and blend on high or use ice cream mode until smooth. Ice cream will be soft. It can be eaten as is or, for firmer ice cream, pour mixture into ice cube trays or plastic bags. If using zip bags, fill three 1-qt bags about ⅔ full, squeeze air out, close & lay flat in the freezer for 6-8 hours or till completely frozen. To serve, re-blend now frozen cubes or bagged ice cream ingredients on high and enjoy.

Mango Ginger Ice Cream 🍶

Makes 4 Cups   Also Veg, V, Grain Free, Egg Free

1	cup **whole** coconut milk
1	cup ripe, sweet mango
⅓	cup raw honey
1	tsp liquid stevia
⅛	tsp sea salt
2½	cups ice cubes (not crushed ice)
2	Tbsp fresh minced ginger root or 1½ tsp ground

If you prefer your Mango Ice Cream without the ginger, you can leave it out. But, remember ginger root has many benefits which include reducing inflammation and exercise-related muscle pain, improving morning sickness and other nausea.

For both the Mango Ginger & Mint Chip ice cream, put all ingredients (except for chopped chocolate) into a **high-speed blender.** Blend on high or use ice cream mode until smooth. Ice cream will be soft. It can be eaten as is or, for firmer ice cream, pour mixture into ice cube trays or plastic bags. If using zip bags, fill 3 1-qt bags about ⅔ full, squeeze air out, close and lay flat in freezer for 6-8 hours or till completely frozen. To serve, re-blend now frozen cubes or bagged ice cream ingredients on high briefly, until evenly blended. (For Mint Chip Ice Cream stir in the chopped chocolate.) Enjoy.

Mangoes are sweetly delicious, low glycemic & contain over 20 vitamins & minerals.

Mint Chip Ice Cream 🍶

Makes 3½ cups   Also Veg, V, Grain Free, Egg Free

¾	cup **whole** coconut milk	⅛	tsp +1/16 tsp sea salt
¼	cup raw honey	1½	cups lightly packed fresh spinach
½	tsp liquid stevia	2½	cups ice cubes (not crushed ice)
1	Tbsp vanilla	¼	cup dark chocolate chips, finely chopped,
¼	tsp peppermint extract		See suggested chocolates in "Stocking Your GF, DF, SF Pantry," p.5

Directions are included in Mango Ginger Ice Cream recipe above.

Sweet Almond Crêpes

Makes Four 6" Crêpes   Also Veg, V, **Grain Free**, Egg Free

Crêpes
- ¾ cup almond **flour**
- ¼ cup tapioca flour
- 1½ tsp coconut flour
- ¼ tsp sea salt
- ¾ cup **whole** coconut milk
- 1½ Tbsp coconut palm sugar
- • coconut oil

Delightfully delicious & Delightfully healthy!

Please note that this recipe calls for almond **flour** which is blanched & is a finer consistency than almond **meal.**

In a small to medium-size bowl, whisk flours and salt together till evenly combined. Stir sugar into milk and whisk till dissolved. Add it to flour mixture. Preheat a nonstick pan, or if using a pan without a nonstick surface, rub pan with a tiny bit of coconut oil and wipe away any extra. For best results, preheat pan 2-3 minutes on medium heat. Pour ¼ of batter into pan. It should sizzle a little at first. Help spread batter using the back of a spoon to make crêpe approximately 6" in diameter and only ¹⁄₁₆" thick. Cook 1½-1¾ minutes, check underneath with a spatula and flip it when underneath side is golden. Cook 2nd side another 1½-1¾ minutes till it is golden. Remove to a plate.

With Chocolate Ganache:
- ¾ cup Chocolate Ganache, p.159
- ½ cup Cashew Whipped "Cream", p.173
- 3 Tbsp chopped pistachios

Spoon 3 Tbsp chocolate ganache across each crêpe and roll them up. Top with a dollop of Cashew Whipped Cream and sprinkle with pistachios.

With Strawberries & Almond Cream Filling:
- 1 lb sliced strawberries
- ¾ cup Almond Cream Filling, recipe below
- ¼ cup sliced almonds
- • chocolate shavings, optional

Stack in this order: 1 crêpe, ¼ of the strawberries, 3 Tbsp Almond Cream filling. Repeat, ending with strawberries on top of last crêpe. Top with a dollop of Almond Cream Filling, sliced almonds & chocolate shavings, if desired.

Almond Cream Filling

Makes 2½ Cups   Also Veg, V, Grain Free, Egg Free

- 1½ cups raw, unsalted cashews
- 1½ cups **light** coconut milk, divided
- ¾ tsp agar **powder**
- 2½ Tbsp raw honey
- ¼ tsp liquid stevia
- ¼ tsp + ⅛ tsp sea salt
- 1 tsp almond extract

Soak the cashews in 2 cups of water for at least 2 hours if your blender is powerful, or longer (4-8 hours) for a less powerful blender. This will cause the nuts to blend into a creamier texture. Rinse the nuts using a wire mesh strainer and drain well on a paper towel. In a 1-qt saucepan, whisk together 1 cup of the milk and the agar powder. Set over medium-low heat and continue stirring with the whisk for 5 minutes as it comes to a boil. Remove from heat. Into a **high-speed blender**, put all of the ingredients including the agar-milk and remaining ½ cup of milk. Blend on high until smooth, scraping sides of blender as needed. Pour into a 2½-3 cup container, cover and refrigerate 3-4 hours. It will continue to firm up.

Use this Almond Cream to turn a simple bowl of fruit, an Almond Walnut Bar, p.143 or an unfrosted slice of Spice Cake, p.163 into delicious new desserts.

Almond Coconut Brittle

Makes 3 Cups   Also Veg, V, Grain Free, Egg Free

- 2 cups toasted, halved almonds
- ⅔ cup unsweetened large flake coconut
- ⅓ cup toasted sunflower seeds
- 2 Tbsp toasted sesame seeds, optional
- ⅓ cup water
- ⅔ cup coconut palm sugar
- ¼ tsp sea salt
- ¼ tsp liquid stevia

Hooray for healthier nut brittle! Sweet, salty, buttery & crunchy, but made with lower glycemic, natural, unrefined sweeteners and, as always, dairy free. This recipe is versatile. You can substitute other nuts in place of the coconut or seeds. Try pepitas, cashews, pistachios...or just the almonds. Only be sure to keep the same ratio of nuts to syrup.

If your almonds or sunflower seeds are not already toasted (which makes them crunchier), toast each as follows: To toast the almonds, spread on a baking sheet and bake 6 minutes at 350°. To toast the sunflower seeds, spread on baking sheet and bake 10 minutes at 350°.

Measure all ingredients before starting. Line a rimmed baking sheet with parchment paper. Preheat oven to 325°. In a 2-qt pot, bring water and sugar to a boil as you stir over medium heat. Boil 1 minute while stirring. Remove from heat. Stir in the salt and stevia. Stir in the nuts, coconut and seeds, and set aside till syrup thickens (about 5 minutes). Stir till well coated. Pour and spread the mixture out onto the parchment-lined baking sheet, making a thin layer. Bake for 16 minutes till bubbly and golden but before it turns brown. Remove from oven and allow to cool completely. Brittle will harden as it cools. Break into pieces and store in a covered container.

Cashew Whipped "Cream" 🫙

Makes 2+ Cups   Also Veg, V, Grain Free, Egg Free

- 1 cup raw, unsalted cashews
- 1½ cups **light** coconut milk, divided
- ¾ tsp agar **powder**
- ¼ tsp liquid stevia*
- 2 Tbsp raw honey
- ¼ tsp sea salt

What tastes like an indulgence of delicious whipped "cream" on the already healthy *Delightfully Free* waffles, hot chocolate, pies & crumbles is also a way to top your treat with a little added low glycemic nutrition.

Soak the cashews in 2 cups of water for at least 2 hours if your blender is powerful, or longer (4-8 hours) for a less powerful blender. This will cause the nuts to blend into a creamier texture. Rinse the nuts using a wire mesh strainer and drain well on a paper towel. In a 1-qt saucepan, whisk together 1 cup of the milk and the agar powder. Set over medium-low heat and continue stirring with the whisk for 5 minutes as it comes to a boil. Remove from heat. Into a **high-speed blender,** put all of the ingredients including the agar-milk and remaining ½ cup of milk. Blend on high until smooth, scraping sides of blender as needed. Pour into a 2½-3 cup container, cover and refrigerate 3-4 hours. It will continue to firm up.

Allow 3-4 hours to chill, then enjoy!

*Be careful adding the stevia. It is very sweet and can overpower this delicate topping. Add only 4-5 drops at a time and taste.

Jesus said to them, "I am the bread of life; whoever comes to Me shall not hunger, and whoever believes in Me shall never thirst." John 6:35

INDEX